Autumn

AUTUMN
KARL OVE KNAUSGAARD

With illustrations by Vanessa Baird
Translated from the Norwegian by Ingvild Burkey

Penguin Press | New York | 2017

PENGUIN PRESS
An imprint of Penguin Random House LLC
375 Hudson Street
New York, New York 10014
penguin.com

Illustrations by Vanessa Baird

Originally published in Norwegian under the title *Om hosten*
by Forlaget Oktober, Oslo

ISBN: 9780399563300 (hardcover)
ISBN: 9780399563317 (e-book)

Printed in the United States of America
10 9 8 7 6 5 4 3 2 1

Letter to an Unborn Daughter 28 August

SEPTEMBER

Apples 9

Wasps 13

Plastic Bags 17

The Sun 21

Teeth 23

Porpoises 25

Petrol 29

Frogs 33

Churches 37

Piss 39

Frames 45

Twilight 47

Beekeeping 51

Blood 53

Lightning 57

Chewing Gum 61

Lime 65

Adders 69

Mouth 73

Daguerrotype 77

Letter to an Unborn Daughter 29 September

OCTOBER

Fever 89

Rubber Boots 91

Jellyfish 93

War 95

Labia 99

Beds 103

Fingers 105

Autumn Leaves 109

Bottles 111

Stubble Fields 115

Badgers 119

Infants 123

Cars 127

Loneliness 129

Experience 131

Lice 135

Van Gogh 139

The Migration of Birds 143

Oil Tankers 145

Earth 149

Letter to an Unborn Daughter 22 October

NOVEMBER

Tin Cans 161

Faces 165

Pain 167

Dawn 171

Telephones 173

Flaubert 177

Vomit 181

Flies 185

Forgiveness 189

Buttons 193

Thermos Flasks 197

The Willow 201

Toilet Bowls 205

Ambulances 207

August Sander 209

Chimneys 211

Bird of Prey 213

Silence 215

Drums 219

Eyes 223

Letter to an Unborn Daughter

28 August. Now, as I write this, you know nothing about anything, about what awaits you, the kind of world you will be born into. And I know nothing about you. I have seen an ultrasound image and have laid my hand on the belly in which you are lying, that is all. Six months remain until you will be born, and anything at all can happen during that time, but I believe that life is strong and indomitable, I think you will be fine, and that you will be born sound and healthy and strong. *See the light of day*, the expression goes. It was night outside when your eldest sister, Vanja, was born, the darkness filled with swirling snow. Just before she came out, one of the midwives tugged at me, *You catch*, she said, and so I did, a tiny child slipped out into my hands, slippery as a seal. I was so happy I cried. When Heidi was born one and a half years later, it was autumn and overcast, cold and damp as October can be, she came out during the morning, labour was rapid, and when her head had emerged but not yet the rest of her body, she made a little sound with her lips, it was such a joyous moment. John, as your big brother is called, came out in a cascade of water and blood, the room had no windows, it felt like we were inside a bunker, and when I went out afterwards to call his two grandparents, I was surprised to

see the light outside, and that life flowed on as if nothing in particular had happened. It was 15 August 2007, it may have been five or six o'clock in the afternoon, in Malmö, where we had moved the previous summer. Later that evening we drove to a patient hotel, and the day after I went to pick up your sisters, who amused themselves greatly by placing a green rubber lizard on top of John's head. They were three and a half and nearly two years old at the time. I took photos, one day I'll show them to you.

That's how they saw the light of day. Now they are big, now they are used to the world, and the strange thing is that they are so unalike, each of them has a personality entirely their own, and they always did, right from the start. I assume that's how it will be with you too, that you already are the person you will become.

Three siblings, a mother and a father, that's us. That's your family. I mention it first because it's what matters most. Good or bad, warm or cold, strict or indulgent, it doesn't matter, this is the most important thing, these are the relationships through which you will come to view your world, and which will shape your understanding of almost everything, directly or indirectly, both in the form of resistance and of support.

Just now, these past few days, we are fine. While the children were at school today, your mother and I went to Lim-hamn, and at a café there, in the late summer heat – today was absolutely marvellous, sun, blue sky, with the faintest hint of autumn in the air, and every colour seemed deep but also bright – we discussed what we are going to call you. I had suggested Anne, if you turn out to be a girl, and now Linda said she really liked the name, there is something light and sunny about it, and that is a quality we want to be associated with you. If you are a boy, your name, we suggested, will be Eirik. Then your name will have the same sound in it as the names of all your three siblings – y – for if you say them out loud, they all have it – Vanja (Vanya), Heidi (Heydi), John (Yonn).

They are asleep now, all four of them. I am sitting in my study, which is actually a little house with two rooms and a loft, looking out across the lawn towards the house where they are lying, the dark windowpanes which would be invisible if not for the street lamps across the road and the light they cast, which fills the kitchen with a faint ghostly glow. The house is really three cottages in a row, converted into one. Two of them are of red-painted wood, one is of whitewashed brick and plaster. Once upon a time families who worked on one of the big farms in the area lived here. Between these two houses there is a guest house, which we call the summer house. Within the horseshoe shape the buildings form there is the garden, which extends for maybe thirty metres to a white wall. There are two plum trees there, an old one, one of the boughs of which has grown so long and so heavy that it has to be supported on two crutches, and a young one I planted last summer, now bearing fruit for the first time, and a pear tree too, also old, much taller than the houses, and three apple trees. One of the apple trees was in pretty bad shape, many of the branches were dead, it seemed stiff and lifeless, but then I pruned it earlier this summer, which I've never done before, and I grew so eager I kept cutting and cutting without stopping to look how it was turning out, until finally, late in the evening, I climbed down and took a few steps back to look at it. *Maimed* was the word that came to mind. But

3

the branches have grown back, densely covered with leaves, and the tree is loaded with apples. That's the experience I've gained from working in the garden: there's no reason to be cautious or anxious about anything, life is so robust, it seems to come cascading, blind and green, and at times it is frightening, because we too are alive, but we live in what amounts to a controlled environment, which makes us fear whatever is blind, wild, chaotic, stretching towards the sun, but most often also beautiful, in a deeper way than the purely visual, for the soil smells of rot and darkness, teems with scuttling beetles and convulsing worms, the flower stalks are juicy, their petals brim with scents, and the air, cold and sharp, warm and humid, filled with sunrays or rain, lies against skin, accustomed to the indoors, like a soothing compress of hereness. Behind the main house lies the road, which ends some hundred metres further on, in a sort of abandoned little semi-industrial area, the buildings have corrugated tin roofs and the windows are broken, engines and axle shafts lie rusting outside, almost disappearing into the grass. On the other side, behind the house in which I am sitting, there is a large farm building made of red brick, it is beautiful to look at, towering up amid the green foliage.

Red and green.

They mean nothing to you, but to me those two colours contain so much, something within them exerts a powerful pull, and I think this is one of the reasons why I have become a writer, for I feel that pull so strongly, and I know that it's important, but I lack the words to express it, and therefore I don't know what it is. I have tried, and I have capitulated. My capitulation is the books I have published. You can read them some day, and maybe you will understand what I mean.

The blood flowing through the veins, the grass growing in the soil, the trees, oh the trees swaying in the wind.

These astounding things, which you will soon encounter and see for yourself, are so easy to lose sight of, and there are almost as many ways of doing that as there are people. That is why I am writing this book for you. I want to show you the world, as it is, all around us, all the time. Only by doing so will I myself be able to glimpse it.

What makes life worth living?

No child asks itself that question. To children life is self-evident. Life goes without saying: whether it is good or bad makes no difference. This is because children don't see the world, don't observe the world, don't contemplate the world, but are so deeply immersed in the world that they don't distinguish between it and their own selves. Not until that happens, until a distance appears between what they are and what the world is, does the question arise: what makes life worth living?

Is it the feeling of pressing down the door handle and pushing the door open, feeling it swing inward or outward on its hinges, always easily and willingly, and entering a new room?

Yes, the door opens, like a wing, and that alone makes life worth living.

To someone who has lived for many years, the door is obvious. The house is obvious, the garden is obvious, the sky and the sea are obvious, even the moon, suspended in the night sky and shining brightly above the rooftops, is obvious. The world expresses its being, but we are not listening, and since we are no longer immersed in it, experiencing it as a part of ourselves, it is as if it escapes us. We open the door, but it doesn't mean anything, it's nothing, just something we do to get from one room to another.

I want to show you our world as it is now: the door, the floor, the water tap and the sink, the garden chair close to the wall beneath the kitchen window, the sun, the water, the trees. You will come to see it in your own way, you will experience things for yourself and live a life of your own, so of course it is primarily for my own sake that I am doing this: showing you the world, little one, makes my life worth living.

SEPTEMBER

Apples

For some reason or other, the fruits that grow in the Nordic countries are easily accessible, with only a thin skin that yields readily covering their flesh, this is true for pears and apples as well as for plums, all one needs to do is bite into them and gobble them down, while the fruits that grow further south, like oranges, mandarins, bananas, pomegranates, mangoes and passion fruit, are often covered with thick, inedible skins. Normally, in accordance with my other preferences in life, I prefer the latter, both because the notion that pleasure must be deserved through prior effort is so strong in me, and because I have always been drawn towards the hidden and the secret. To bite a piece of the peel from the top of an orange in order to work one's thumb in between the peel and the flesh of the orange, and feel the bitter taste spurting into one's mouth for a brief second, and then to loosen piece after piece, sometimes, if the peel is thin, in tiny scraps, other times, when the peel is thick and loosely connected to the flesh, in one long piece, also has a ritual aspect to it. It is almost as if first one is in the temple colonnade and moving slowly towards the innermost room, but there the teeth pierce the thin, shiny membrane and the fruit juice runs into the mouth and fills it with sweetness. Both the labour involved and the fruit's secretive nature, by which I mean its inaccessibility, increase the value of the pleasure one experiences. The apple is an exception to this. All one has to do is reach up a hand, grab the apple and sink one's teeth into it. No work, no secret, just straight into pleasure, the almost explosive release of the apple's sharp, fresh and tart yet always sweet taste into the mouth, which may cause the nerves to twinge and maybe also the facial muscles to contract, as if the distance between man and fruit is just big enough for this shock on a miniature scale to never quite disappear, regardless of how many apples one has eaten in one's life.

When I was a fairly small child, I began to eat the whole apple. Not just the flesh, but the core with all the pips in it, even the stem. Not because it tasted good, I don't think, nor because of any idea I might have had that I shouldn't be wasteful, but because eating the core and the stem presented an obstacle to pleasure. It was work of a kind, even if in reverse order: first the reward, then the effort. It is still unthinkable for me to throw away an apple core, and when I see my children doing it – sometimes they even throw away half-eaten apples – I am filled with indignation, but I don't say anything, because I want them to relish life and to have a sense of its abundance. I want them to feel that living is easy. And this is why I've changed my attitude towards apples, not through an act of will, but as a result of having seen and understood more, I think, and now I know that it is never really about the world in itself, merely about our way of relating to it. Against secrecy stands openness, against work stands freedom. Last Sunday we went to the beach about ten kilometres from here, it was one of those early autumn days which summer had stretched into and saturated almost completely with its warmth and calm, yet the tourists had gone home long ago and the beach lay deserted. I took the children for a walk in the forest, which grows all the way down to the edge of the sand, and which for the most part consists of deciduous trees, with the occasional red-trunked pine. The air was warm and still, the sun hung heavy with light on the faintly dark blue sky. We followed a path in between the trees, and there, in the middle of the wood, stood an apple tree laden with apples. The children were as astonished as I was, apple trees are supposed to grow in gardens, not wild out in the forest. Can we eat them, they asked. I said yes, go ahead, take as many as you want. In a sudden glimpse, as full of joy as it was of sorrow, I understood what freedom is.

Wasps

The body of a wasp is divided into two parts, of which the hindmost is shaped something like a faintly rounded cone, with a smooth and shiny surface, while the front part is more spherical and only a third of the length of the hind part, and yet the legs, the wings and the antennae all extend from the front. With its yellow and black pattern, shiny surface and rounded conical shape, the hind part resembles a tiny Easter egg, or maybe a miniature Fabergé egg, for if one looks closely, it is striking how regular and beautiful the pattern is; the black stripes divide up the field of yellow like slender ribbons, and where the black dots lie adjacent to the stripes, they resemble painstakingly painted decorative borders. Its hardness – which to us seems not very great, it takes no more than a slight pressure of the fingers for the shell to crack and the soft innards to ooze out, but which must seem like armour plating in the world of the wasp – brings to mind a suit of armour, and when the wasp comes flying, with its six legs, two pairs of wings and two antennae, it is almost like a knight dressed for battle. This is what I thought last week, when the weather was splendid and summery and I decided to seize the opportunity and paint the west wall of the house. I knew there had to be a wasps' nest inside the air vent, for we could often hear buzzing behind the wall when we went to bed in the evening, and it stopped just where the wasps crawled in, and sometimes a few of them even got into the room, though both the window and the door were shut. As I put the ladder up and, with paint can and brush in one hand, climbed far enough to reach the boards below the eaves, I didn't give them a thought, for even though they dwelled only a few feet from our bed, they had never turned against us, it was as if we didn't exist to them or were only a part of the backdrop they lived their lives against. But this afternoon that changed. As soon as I started painting, I heard a faint scratching sound from the air vent and a wasp came crawling out, took off from the edge and with a buzz flew up maybe twenty metres into the air, where it was no more than a tiny speck against the vast blue of the sky, before it came diving straight at me at the same time as another wasp came crawling out of the air vent, and another and another. All in all five wasps circled around me. I tried shooing them away with my left hand, carefully so as not to fall, but of course that didn't help at all. They didn't sting me, but their aggressive movements and their angry buzzing were enough to make me climb down and light a cigarette as I pondered what to do. There was something humiliating about my situation, compared to me they were so tiny, no bigger than my outermost finger joints, and considerably thinner. I fetched the fly swatter from the kitchen and climbed back up. No sooner had I dipped the brush into the oily red paint and applied the first strokes than I heard the scratching noise again. Soon the first wasp was out on the edge of the vent and letting itself drop down into the air before circling me; shortly afterwards I was surrounded again. I struck out at them and hit a couple, but only in mid-air, and all that happened was they were knocked off course. I hardly got any painting done. I gave up, poured the paint back into the larger can and cleaned the brush. A few hours later I climbed the ladder as gently as I could, sealed the air vent with gaffer tape, tiptoed down again, hurried inside up to the bedroom, where I taped shut the inside of the vent as well. When we went to bed that evening, the buzzing outside didn't cease. Nor the evening after. But then it went quiet.

Plastic Bags

Since plastic takes such an extremely long time to decompose, since the number of plastic bags in the world is so huge and just keeps increasing with every passing day, and since they are so light and can catch the wind both like a sail and like a balloon, one comes across plastic bags in the most unexpected places. Yesterday, as I parked the car after a trip to the shop, a plastic bag was flapping from the roof of the house, the handle had snagged on the climbing plant that grows there. And some days before that, when I was going to plant four redcurrant bushes I had bought and was digging holes for them a few metres from the fence at one end of the garden, I struck a layer of broken roof tiles and strips of plastic, which I realised from the printed logo must be shopping bags. How they had ended up there I don't know, but there was something disturbing about the sight of them, for the thin plastic, so white and smooth against the black and crumbling mould, was so obviously a foreign substance. That property soil has of transforming everything that ends up in it into itself does not apply to plastic, which is made in such a way that it repels everything: the soil slides over the surface of the plastic, finding no hold, no place to penetrate, and the same goes for water. The plastic bag has something inviolable about it, it seems to exist in a place beyond everything else, including time and its inexorable modality. I felt a stab of sorrow at the sight of the buried bags without quite understanding why. It may have been the thought of pollution, it may have been the thought of death, but it may also have been the thought that I wouldn't be able to plant the redcurrants there after all. Presumably it was all of these at once. As I pushed the shovel down with my foot into the soil a bit further away and began digging a hole there, I reflected on why nearly all my thoughts and associations ran in that direction, ending in problems and worries and darkness instead of in joy, ease and light. One of the most beautiful things I have ever seen was a plastic bag adrift in the water beyond a jetty on an island far out at sea, so why hadn't that come to mind instead? The water had been perfectly limpid, the way it gets when it is cold and still, with a faint cool green tinge to it, and the plastic bag had hung at a depth of maybe ten feet, distended and motionless. It resembled nothing other than itself, no creature, no jellyfish, nor a hot-air balloon, it was just a plastic bag. Yet I remained standing there, looking at it. This was on Sandøya, the outermost of the group of islands known as Bulandet, which lies far out to sea beyond the west coast of Norway. Besides me, only three people lived there. The air was freezing cold, the sky blue, the jetty I was standing on was partly covered with snow. I used to go there every day, attracted by that sub-aquatic world, down into which chains and mooring lines disappeared, its limpidity and inaccessibility. The starfish, the clustered shells, the seaweed, but most of all the space they appeared in, the sea, which on the other side of the island struck the land in long heavy rollers but which here was calm between the walls of smooth rock and the cement quay above the sandy floor of the harbour basin, which it filled with its transparency. Or, the water wasn't completely transparent, it distorted the light slightly, rather like thick glass, so that the white plastic bag, which for the entire time that I stood there hung absolutely motionless midway between the surface and the bottom, gleamed with a faint greenish hue and lacked the sharpness that white plastic possesses on land, in daylight, when there is only air between it and the light, but rather seemed faintly obscured and somehow softened.

Why could I hardly take my eyes off the submerged plastic bag?

The sight did not fill me with joy, I did not come away feeling happy. Nor was I filled with contentment when I caught sight of it, it wasn't that something stilled within me, as hunger or thirst do when they are satisfied. But it felt good to look at it, the way it feels good to read a poem that ends in an image of something concrete and seems to fasten on it, so that the inexhaustible within it can unfold calmly. Swollen with water, handles up, the plastic bag hung a few feet down in the water on this February day in 2002. This moment was not the beginning of anything, not even of an insight, nor was it the conclusion of anything, and maybe that is what I was thinking as I stood digging holes in the ground a few days ago, that I was still in the middle of something and always would be.

The Sun

Every single day since I was born the sun has been there, but somehow I've never quite got used to it, perhaps because it is so unlike everything else we know. The sun is one of the few phenomena in our existence that we are unable to get close to, if we did we would be obliterated, nor can we dispatch probes, satellites or spacecraft there, they too would be destroyed. That we cannot even look directly at the sun without being blinded or having our eyesight permanently damaged sometimes feels like an unreasonable restriction, even an insult: right above us, visible to every human being and animal all over the world, an enormous fiery orb hangs suspended, and we can't even *look* at it! But that's how it is. If we look straight at the sun for only a few seconds, the retina fills with small quivering black spots, and if we fix our gaze on it, the blackness spreads across the inside of our eyes like ink on blotting paper. Above us, then, hangs a blazing ball which not only provides us with all our light and warmth but is also the origin and source of all life, while at the same time it is absolutely unapproachable and completely indifferent to its creation. It is difficult to read about the monotheistic god of the Old Testament without thinking of the sun. An essential characteristic of man's relation to God is that human beings may not look directly at God but must bow their heads. And the very image of God's presence in the Bible is fire, it represents the divine but also and always the sun since every flame and all fires here on earth are offshoots of it. God is the unmoved mover, Thomas Aquinas wrote, and Dante, his contemporary, described divinity as a river of light, and ended *La Divina Commedia* with a glimpse of God himself, in the form of an eternally shining circle. In this way human beings under the sun, who without religion were merely arbitrary creatures and slaves to their condition, gained enormous significance, and the sun became no more than a star. But while conceptions of reality rise and fall, flare up and fade away, reality itself is unyielding, its conditions immutable: day dawns in the east, slowly darkness yields its ground, and while the air fills with birdsong, sunlight strikes the back of the clouds, which change from grey to pink to shining white, while the sky that only minutes before was greyish-black now turns blue and the first rays fill the garden with light. It is day. People walk to and from their daily tasks, the shadows grow shorter and shorter, then longer and longer, as the earth turns. When we eat dinner outside, beneath the apple tree, the air is full of children's voices, the clatter of cutlery, the rustle of leaves in the mild breeze, and no one notices that the sun is hanging right above the roof of the guest house, no longer blazing yellow but orange, burning silently.

Teeth

When the first teeth appear, these little stones slowly pushed up through the child's red gums, appearing at first like sharp little points, then standing there like miniature white towers in the mouth, it is hard not to be astonished, for where do they come from? Nothing that enters the baby, mostly milk but also a little mashed banana and potato, bears the slightest resemblance to teeth, which in contrast to the food are hard. Yet this must be what happens – that certain substances are extracted from this partly liquid, partly soft nourishment and transported to the jaws, where they are assembled into the material used to make teeth. But how? That skin and flesh, nerves and sinews are formed and grow is perhaps just as great a mystery, but it doesn't feel that way. The tissue is soft and living, the cells stand open to each other and to the world in a relationship of exchange. Light, air and water pass through them in human beings and animals as well as in plants and trees. But teeth are entirely closed, impervious to everything, and seem nearer to the mineral world of mountains and rock, gravel and sand. So what really is the difference between rocks formed by hardening lava and then eroded by wind and weather over millions of years, or formed by infinitely slow processes of sedimentation, where something originally soft is compressed until it becomes hard as diamond, and these little enamelled stones, which at this very moment are pushing up through the jaws of my children as they lie asleep in the dark of their rooms? To the oldest two, growing and losing teeth has become routine. But the youngest one still finds it a source of great excitement. Losing your first tooth is an event, also your second and perhaps even your third, but then inflation sets in, and the teeth seem to just drop out, loosening in the evening in bed, so that next morning I have to ask why there are bloodstains on the pillow, or in the afternoon in the living room while eating an apple, and it's no longer a big deal. 'Here, Daddy,' one of them might say, handing me the tooth, which I close my hand around and carry into the kitchen. What am I supposed to do with it? I stand in front of the kitchen counter, the muted light of the autumn sky beyond the windows shines faintly on the tap and sink in front of me. The little tooth, sharply white, dark red with blood at the root, is thrown into almost obscenely sharp relief against my pinkish palm. It feels wrong to throw it away. The tooth is a part of her. And yet I can't keep it, for what are we going to do with it? Put it in a box full of tiny rattling teeth to take out when we are old and reminisce about who they were then? Teeth don't age in the same way as the rest of the body, they are impervious even to time; in this tooth she will stay ten years old for ever. I open the cupboard under the sink and drop the tooth into the waste bin, where it lands on top of a damp coffee filter, turned grey by the black coffee grounds still inside it. I take a crumpled muesli bag and place it on top, so that the tooth is no longer visible.

Porpoises

We were out on the fjord in the rowing boat, the sky was grey and heavy. Before us lay Lihesten, a long, almost vertical cliff which rises straight from the fjord to a height of several hundred metres, in some places visible as a darker, slate-coloured wall deep in the fog. My hair was damp. If I ran my finger over the sleeve of my waterproof jacket, water gathered along it. The creaking and knocking of the oars against the rowlocks could be heard more distinctly than usual; the sounds that normally left the boat and dissipated across the open water were now held back, packed in close by the fog, which also prevented other sounds from reaching us. When my grandfather stopped rowing and pulled in the oars, everything went quiet. The water moved slowly, in great undulating swells, the surface was almost completely smooth. My cousin and I let out the sinkers, which spun down into the deep beneath us. Then a sort of rushing noise came from somewhere nearby. My cousin looked up. Grandfather didn't react at first. The sound grew louder, a faint ripple added itself to the rushing sound, something moved through the water. My cousin pointed, grandfather turned to look. Just a few metres away the necks and backs of a pod of sea animals rose from and sank back into the water.

I felt something lift within me.

There were five, six of them, they were swimming close together, ploughing through the water, which whitened slightly every time they broke the surface. I will always remember that rushing sound. And the sight of them, how they glided past us in the water, with movements that seemed cheerful and concentrated at the same time. Their smooth greyish-brown skin, their blunt bodies the length of children, the glimpse of what must have been their eyes, little black circles above their prominent snouts. And their mouths, which seemed to be smiling.

Later, when they were out of sight, grandfather said that seeing porpoises brings luck. He would say things like that, he believed in omens and signs, but even though I liked hearing it, I didn't believe for a second that it might actually be true. Now I do. For what do we really know about how luck and misfortune are distributed? If they originate within the human realm, as most people seem to think in our rational era – that we ourselves create our own happiness or misfortune – the question becomes what 'ourselves' might mean in a time like ours, if not a mere collection of cells that have realised an inherited trait and been modified by experience, and that are activated and deactivated in tiny electrochemical storms, causing us to feel, think, say, do something in particular? The external consequences of which set off a new inner storm and a subsequent series of emotions, thoughts, statements, actions? Such a reduction is absurd and mechanistic, but no more absurd and mechanistic than the reduction of porpoises to marine mammals with certain traits and patterns of behaviour, for anyone who has experienced them, rising not only out of the deep, but out of time itself, unchanged as they have been for millions of years, knows that to see them is to be moved by something: it is as if they are touching you, as if you have thereby been chosen.

Petrol

On rainy days in autumn, when the sky was dark grey, the spruce trees in the forest along the road dark green and the asphalt on the road black, and all other colours were dulled by the restrained light and the humidity, petrol sometimes lay on the road surface shimmering in the most fantastic and unusual colours. Petrol was so unlike anything else we knew that it could have come from another world. A magnificent world full of adventure, one had to imagine, brightly coloured and bountiful. Bountiful because the petrol's play of colours, which appeared and disappeared seemingly at random, was connected to the emptiest and ugliest of places. Its iridescence was never found in meadows or fields, on smooth rock slopes or sandy beaches, but turned up on parking lots, gravel and asphalt roads, small-boat marinas, construction sites. On the yellowish-grey surface of puddles made opaque by gravel dust petrol could suddenly float, unconnected to the water as well as to anything else in its surroundings, and if you poked a stick into it, new colours could emerge – scarlet, purple, royal blue – in swirling patterns full of eddies and lagoons, beautiful as conches or galaxies. They were a mystery in themselves, those volatile, mirage-like convolutions of colour, and they were like an image of the mystery. Not least because everyone knew that petrol actually had no colour. All of us had seen petrol being poured from a jerrycan through a funnel into a red fuel tank in one of the boats by the floating docks. The petrol was then completely colourless and transparent, but at the same time it caused the surrounding air to tremble. And we all knew the vast power it possessed. The huge bulldozers that cleared the blasting sites of rubble, which simply rammed their blades straight into the rocks, lifted them as they backed up, and then dumped them clattering down into the bed of a waiting truck, they were powered by petrol, and the heavy-laden truck that soon drove out onto the road ran on petrol, and the articulated lorries and the buses and the oil tankers and the airplanes. The racing boats that seemed almost to fly above the waves out in the sound were powered by petrol, and the racing cars which we read about but had never seen. Not to mention our parents' cars, those wide conveyances that swayed along the roads every day, and the motorcycles and mopeds that the youths rode. The snowploughs, the tractors, the excavators, the chainsaws, the outboard engines. All the speed and power that surrounded us, all the roaring, thundering, chugging engines burned petrol. That petrol was extracted from crude oil, which was brought up from reservoirs deep under the ground and consisted of transformed organic matter from a time when human beings didn't exist, only dinosaurs, those gigantic but simple creatures, and when trees and plants too were larger and simpler, and that it was the prehistoric force of that zoological and biological matter which now unfolded around us, all this made sense – the kinship between the bulldozer and the dinosaur was obvious to any child – but not the connection between the power of petrol and the mysterious beauty of the small trembling rainbow swirls in the many puddles of the 1970s.

Frogs

This summer we attended a sixtieth-birthday celebration. It was held in a function hall near a fjord in western Norway, not far from the sea. It had rained all day, and it was raining as we left for home late in the evening. We trotted down the muddy gravel track towards the car, I put our bags in the boot while the children, dazed with fatigue and boredom, buckled up inside the large minivan I had rented for the week. The rain pelted down on the dark landscape. The darkness was of the kind that only occurs under just such conditions, for usually the summer nights here are light, as if barely veiled by darkness, which isn't black but bluish and somehow insubstantial. The fog and the heavy clouds, which had lain like a lid over the trough between the mountains all day long, gave the darkness a density, but it wasn't total, it still wasn't black, for through the dark grey and humid air the spruces could still be glimpsed around us, and *they* were black as night.

I started the car, put the headlights on full beam and drove down to the narrow asphalt road. It ran along the fjord and was so narrow that I had to brake whenever another car approached and sometimes reverse to the nearest passing place, and in some places the only safeguard against the steep slopes and the precipitous mountainsides were old-fashioned roadside guard stones. The headlights opened up the darkness ahead of us and made it seem as if we were driving through an endless tunnel. The road left the fjord, rose up through a valley, over a mountain, and down on the other side it joined yet another fjord, which it followed for twenty kilometres or so.

There, little stones began to appear on the asphalt. My daughter, who was sitting motionless next to me, staring at the road as if hypnotised by the light in the darkness, suddenly said that the stones were moving. As soon as she said this, I saw it too. They were moving across the tarmac with little hops. They weren't stones, they were frogs. And there were more and more of them. In some places there were maybe thirty, forty of them on the asphalt ahead of us. It was impossible to dodge them all; in places where they were very close together I was forced to drive right over them. For several kilometres they just kept coming, hundreds of them, all of them came crawling up from the ditch that night, hopped across the road and down the other side. Was it because of the rain? Or was it the time of year, that on one particular night every summer they all moved together to a new area? I would probably never know, I thought as we drove in rain and darkness along the twisting road above the fjord. Like all other amphibians there was something primordial about them, they came from a different time than us, from a world that was simpler, for even trees and plants were more primitive then, and that they were still here, unlike nearly all the other creatures that had existed at that time, was due to the fact that their way of life was so resilient and unaffected by all the changes the surrounding world had undergone. To them the world now must appear the exact same as the world then: they saw, did, thought and felt the same, and this changelessness, in which neither the past nor the future existed, was in principle no different from that possessed by more recent species, like squirrels or badgers, except that it had lasted immeasurably longer. And yet it was a shock to see them at close range, like that time I went on a walk in the woods with my daughters' kindergarten class, and suddenly among the leaves there were lots of little leaping frogs. One of the parents caught one and held it up in his hand for the children to see. There was something repulsive about it, and I thought it must be the eyes, which contained everything we associate with evil. They were cold and empty, they didn't open onto a soul, as for example the eyes of a cat do. Those eyes did not see people, but something else; precisely what we will never know.

Churches

From the ridge above Glemmingebro, where we live, three churches are visible in the landscape. One built of red brick and with a copper-coloured tower, that is Glemminge church, which dates back to the turn of the last century, when the old church was torn down, having become too small for the growing community, and two from the Middle Ages, whitewashed and towerless, those are Ingelstorp church and Valleberga church. They were built at a time when each little village formed a separate unit, with the low houses clustering around the church like ducklings around a mother duck, surrounded by fields in every direction, and while this pattern remains the same, it no longer means anything, but testifies to a bygone way of life and thinking. Nothing is gathered in one place any more, as the church used to symbolise, a building where baptism, confirmation, marriage and funeral rites were enacted for the villagers, who gathered there every Sunday in the rituals of the sedentary beneath an immutable sky. The soil here is among the most fertile in Europe, and the climate is favourable, a combination which once meant wealth; even the smallest village boasted its own church. Today the wealth is in the cities; out here there are vacant houses for sale everywhere at depressed prices.

Shops, libraries and schools are being closed. The land is still cultivated, but with low margins and by only a small number of farmers. That is what I think about as I drive through the landscape, how almost everything I see is more or less the same as it must have been in the nineteenth century. Churches, villages, far-flung fields, great leafy trees, the sky, the sea. And yet everything is different. The sorrow I feel over this is not only groundless, since I have no experience of life in the nineteenth century, it also dampens any joy arising from what is, what we have, to such an extent that it could be categorised as an illness. Nostalgia, the longing for what once was, the shadow sickness. The corresponding natural emotion is the longing for that which still doesn't exist, the future, which is filled with hope and vigour and which is not impossible, not associated with what has been lost but with what can still be gained. And maybe that is why the nostalgia I feel is so powerful, because utopia has vanished from our time, so that longing can no longer be directed forward, but only backwards, where all its force accumulates. Seen in this light, the churches were also feats of spiritual engineering, for not only were they a visualisation of local identity, they also represented another level of reality, the divine, which was present in the midst of everyday toil, and there stood open to the future, when the kingdom of heaven would be established on earth. That no one seeks the divine level of reality any more and that the churches stand empty means that it is no longer necessary. That it is no longer necessary means that the kingdom of heaven has come. There is nothing left to long for other than longing itself, of which the empty churches I can see from here have become the symbol.

Piss

Of all the things we do, pissing is one of the most routine. At the time of writing this I have been alive for roughly 16,500 days. If we assume that I have pissed on average five times on each of these days, the total number of times that I have pissed comes to about 75,000. Not once have I wondered at the phenomenon, not once has it felt alien to me, as one may feel about other bodily functions and phenomena – for example, one's heartbeat or thought impulses – even though for the body pissing is a singular act, since it connects it to the outside world, which through pissing becomes something that flows through us. No, I just position myself in front of the toilet bowl and piss down into the water, which slowly changes both colour and consistency: from being clear and transparent, it turns faintly yellowish green or a dark brown-yellow, depending on how concentrated the piss is, and becomes full of little bubbles. The fragrance which wafts up from the bowl smells faintly of salt, and then there is something else in it, something slightly acrid, stronger when the piss is concentrated than when it is diluted, and which, when many people have pissed in the same place and the actual liquid has evaporated or has seeped down into the ground, forms a wall of stench. This stench, so pungent and so rank that it is unbearable for more than a few seconds at a time, tells us something about the power of crowds, for even if one person's piss contributes to the rankness, it is there only as a suggestion, something almost imperceptible, which it is therefore also possible to find pleasure in. The little stench in one's own piss stands in roughly the same relation to the great stench as the single cigarette does to death: it produces a faint titillation.

But no matter how routinely we piss, and how easy it is, even pissing must be learned. Everyone who has been responsible for the care of an infant knows what it is like when pissing is not controlled: the child lies there on the changing table, and suddenly a shiny golden rivulet begins to trickle out of the crevice between its legs if it is a girl-child, or a shiny golden fountain-like spurt rises from the boy-child's little nozzle, while they gaze indifferently up into the air, smiling or burbling as if what just happened had nothing to do with them. Only a few years later peeing one's pants, as it is called, becomes something shameful to them. Where the shame comes from, I don't know. My experience is that it appears no matter how casually and matter-of-factly the incident is handled. Maybe it isn't the incident in itself which is shameful, but the feelings it fills them with, of not being whole, of not being delimited and autonomous – as an invisible and inaudible but nevertheless powerful and abso-lute demand on them – but something formless, oozing, uncontrolled. The last time I peed myself was surprisingly late, which is why I still remember it in detail. I was fifteen years old and in the ninth grade. We were on a school ski trip in the mountains doing the elective class in outdoor life. It was late winter, February, March, and when we got to the cabin that night a competition sprang up: who could eat the most tins of pineapple? I won, but winning had a price, I was so stuffed with pineapple and pineapple juice that I could hardly walk, and I still have a problem with both the taste and the smell of it. Eventually we lay down to sleep, twelve young boys and girls in their sleeping bags on the floor in the open loft. I woke up in the middle of the night because I had peed myself. My underpants and long johns were soaked through. I was terrified when I realised what had happened. If this were to come out, no greater catastrophe could be imagined. I was fifteen, in love with one of the girls there, and I had peed myself. Gingerly, I extracted myself from the sleeping bag, also wet, and on my knees I opened my backpack and took out a new pair of underpants and a towel. The light of the full moon seeped in through the window. Everyone was breathing heavily around me as I tiptoed across the room and down to the ground floor. I opened the door carefully and went out. Stars sparkled in the sky above me, the moonlight shone on the snow, which stretched out in every direction. I walked to the end of the cabin, undressed, dried my wet thighs and crotch with the towel, put on the fresh pair of underpants and rubbed the damp bundle of piss-drenched underwear in the snow over and over again, found a plastic bag in the kitchen, put the clothes in it, climbed back up and lay down again, after first placing my last towel over the frisbee-sized stain inside the sleeping bag. When I realised that no one had seen me and that no one would ever find out what had happened, the shock and shame disappeared and was replaced by a powerful but peculiar feeling of joy, for once the shame was gone, I could indulge in the vague yet distinct sensation I had had in my sleep: oh God, how delicious it is to pee yourself.

Frames

Frames form the edges of a picture and mark the boundary between what is in the picture and what is not. The frame itself is not a part of the picture, but neither is it a part of what is outside it, the wall on which the picture hangs. Frames never appear on their own in any meaningful way, a frame without a picture is empty, the shape of nothing. The picture frame is closely related to the window frame and the spectacle frame, and more distantly to the wall, the fence, the enclosure, the border, the category. The physical frame, usually of wood, is made to measure by a frame maker or produced in a frame factory. But frame and framework are also used figuratively, to denote that which limits something, such as the time and money spent on a construction project. We speak of time frames and financial frameworks, or religious rites, which take place within the confines of a ritual frame. In other words, the frame limits a phenomenon, sharply demarcates an inside and an outside, and by isolating it, the phenomenon becomes clearly defined, that is it becomes something in itself. It gains an identity. Identity is being one thing and not the other.

In nature there are no frames, all things and phenomena merge into one another, the earth is round, the universe is infinite and time is eternal. What this entails, it has been given to no one to understand, for to be human is to categorise, subdivide, identify and define, to limit and to frame. That is true of our own lives, which we spend largely in our homes, precisely demarcated from the rest of the world by ceilings, floors, walls, and beyond that, if we live in a house, by the boundaries of the property. It is true of our own selves, which we associate with the body and its limits, and with a certain set of thoughts, notions, ideas, opinions and experiences. And it is true of our reality, what we call the world, which we subdivide into objects, groups of objects, phenomena and groups of phenomena, which we conceive of in terms of how they differ from other objects and phenomena. This division is a frame, it creates an inside and an outside, and is not itself perceived as part of the seen or comprehended reality.

These frames, without which neither we nor the world can be conceived, are found in all areas of existence, they apply not only to what is, but also to what ought to be, for the way we behave has definite limits too. Since life is in constant motion, from time to time a divergence arises between what we ought to do and what we want to do, which manifests itself in an urge to go beyond the boundaries that have been set for us. If that urge is given outlet, there follows a period of boundlessness, before life is fixed within new limits. In the life of the individual this is called teenage rebellion, and in the life of the culture it is called generational revolt or revolution or war. Common to all these is the longing for authenticity, for the real, which is simply the place where one's notions about reality and reality itself are one and the same thing. Or in other words, a life, an existence, a world unframed.

Twilight

As I write this, twilight is falling outside. It is no longer possible to discern the colour of the grass or the wooden wall of the house across the lawn, only the whitewashed wall still reflects a little light and is grey-white. The sky above the roofs is lighter; it is down here at the bottom that dusk falls first. Some thirty metres beyond the roofs, up along the road that runs past the churchyard, seven large trees stand with their splayed-out branches. Every smallest detail in the network formed by their branches is visible against the lighter backdrop. When I again turn my attention to the grass, it is already impossible to see; the darkness lies upon it like a small lake. Yet at the same time the rooms of the house seem to emerge from the dark, the yellow light that fills them shines brighter and brighter through the windows. There are six children in there tonight; the smallest has just gone to bed with a bottle of milk between her hands, she is probably asleep now. The six- and seven-year-old are presumably sitting upstairs on the bed playing on their iPads and talking loudly about what they are doing. The two eight-year-olds, who were just now clambering onto a fence at the garden's edge and from there up into a tree, I expect are sitting in the living room watching TV, while the ten-year-old, who just came home from a friend's house, has lain down in bed on the first floor to play Sims. That the light outside is waning is not something they think about. To them this is just one evening among all the others in the endless row that makes up the sum of their childhood. For a couple of weeks they may well be able to remember some of it – that we had lasagne for dinner, for instance – but then it will vanish from memory for ever. Though it isn't always easy to know what will lodge in the mind. This weekend I walked about town with my eight-year-old, and she started telling me what she could remember from when she 'was small', as she put it. It was mostly small details and glimpses of things that she herself did not always know the origin of, whether it was Malmö, Stockholm, Jølster or one of the places we have gone on holiday. A railing with ocean behind it, a small train which ran through a museum, a bench in a forest, where she had eaten her packed lunch. From the apartment in Malmö, where she lived from when she was one till she was five, it was the step up to the veranda door in the bedroom that she remembered and described, where she had sat once.

During the time it has taken to write this, two mothers have been here to collect their children, and the darkness outside is total; everything is black. The only things giving off light are the rooms behind the windows, which from here, inside the little house that I am sitting in, look like aquariums. Beneath the lamp in the dining room I can see the head of the six-year-old, it is bent forward, he is probably watching an episode of a TV series on the iPad. My eight-year-old has just been in the kitchen, and from her movements I guessed that she was spreading something on a slice of bread. Soon I will get up and walk over to them, turn the TV off to protests, tell them to brush their teeth and finally read to them. Then they will close their eyes and lie in the dark waiting for sleep, the bridge that will lead them into tomorrow, while I end this text, about how the twilight hour elapsed here, in Glemmingebro, on Monday the 15th of September 2013.

Animal husbandry partly involves orienting animals towards the human world, for instance by including them in human communication – one smacks one's lips and the horse begins to trot, one sings mournful calls and the cows come in for the night, one says sit and the dog goes down on its haunches – and partly involves orienting the human world towards animals, that is by sheltering them and taking care of their needs. Building stalls for cows, giving them hay and feed and water, clearing out the muck, riding horses, exercising dogs, petting cats. In all animal husbandry there is a zone that lies between humans and animals, where they meet. In a few exceedingly rare cases no meeting occurs, the approach is one-sided, the human being meets the animal and fulfils its needs, but the animal does not meet the human, and the question is whether this can still properly be called animal husbandry, or whether it is something else. Mink farming is one such borderline case. The mink receives food, water and warmth, but is aggressive and frightened, nothing in it has been cowed into submission to the human world; given the chance, it will bite the hand that feeds it or escape its cage and flee into the forest. The mink is more prisoner than domestic animal. It fears the human. Beekeeping is also a borderline case, but for a different reason. Bees are unaware that they are encompassed within the human world, with its caretaking, plans and considerations of exchange. Beekeeping involves recreating bees' natural surroundings to the greatest degree possible, so as to have access to and control over their product, honey, and preventing them from escaping from the hive. Though escape is the wrong word, since it presupposes a will to get away, whereas for bees what is involved is a natural instinct to swarm, which it is then the beekeeper's task to dull or divert. Communication with bees is entirely one-sided: while the beekeeper relates to the bees and constructs an artificial world for them, the bees relate only to each other and their own bee reality. If the beekeeper is unlucky or unskilled and in one way or other breaks the illusion, the bees will leave the hive in a massive swarm and rebuild their community somewhere else. The problem for the beekeeper is that nothing can be offered to the bees that they are unable to procure for themselves, they are entirely self-sufficient, and that they should settle in this particular place, the beekeeper's boxes, is not a given. When the beekeeper pulls out the honey-laden frames it is as any other intruder, who must expect to be stung. To make this special form of animal husbandry possible, the beekeeper has developed a unique sensibility and has got as close to the bees' reality as a human being can. This is what we see when, dressed in their white smocks and white hats and with their faces covered by protective veils, beekeepers carefully and with alien movements work their hives out in the field, in that slow, peculiar dance which shows human beings at their most subservient and perhaps also at their most beautiful.

Blood

Most of the body's interior, its organs and moist cavities, is pale in colour. In some places almost entirely colourless, like the brain's grey, in other places vague, watery, cloudy hues. This colour palette is typical of things that grow inside other things or beneath them. The flesh of seashells, maggots in the soil, clumps of seaweed under water. The exception to this rule, in the body's interior, is the blood, which with its fresh, strong and bright red seems to come from the outside, and to be more akin to the unquestioning green of grass and the sky's blue than to the murky grey-beige-brown of the intestinal wall. When I was smaller, I thought of the body as a kind of receptacle for blood, and that there were large accumulations of it in the body's interior, perhaps precisely because the colour of blood has dignity of quite another order to the colours of the rest of the body, which thereby appear second-rate and subordinate, rather like the way the grey colour of the pail is obviously second-rate and subordinate to the milk's white, and obviously its servant. Now I know that blood makes up a relatively minor portion of the body's total volume, and that nowhere is it found in large pools or channels, but on the contrary is characterised by its dispersal into tiny vessels, and that these permeate the entire body, like a kind of web, through which all manner of nutrients and gases are transported. Like everything else found inside the body, with the partial exception of the brain, the blood doesn't know what it is doing. It is in continuous motion, propelled through the blood vessels by the beating of the heart, and percolating through the flesh in its capillaries. When we see blood, it is often because something in the external world has gone wrong. The sickle slipped off the onion and sliced into the finger on a September evening in a large cold building with bins of potatoes, carrots and onions, and the red blood gushed out, gathering in large drops which dripped onto the concrete floor. The little girl climbed up on the chair, which fell over backwards, and her face struck the floor so that her mouth filled with blood. On a sultry night in August, after lightning had filled the entire sky above the city for several hours, and thunderclap after thunderclap had sounded, two sisters had nosebleeds, they were lying asleep in a bunk bed, and both the white pillowcase and the duvet cover with the Moomin motif were soaked in red.

Seeing blood appear can be a trifling matter, it can be disturbing, and it can be catastrophic. That blood and death are so often connected might have led to red becoming the colour of death, but that's not how it is, black is the colour of death in Western cultures, linked to night and nothingness, while red, on the contrary, is the colour of life and love. Few things are more beautiful than the sight of blood suffusing a confused young person's face and colouring his or her cheeks red as they meet the gaze of another young person.

Unless it be the green grass as it turns red beneath a blue sky, stained by the blood of the dying hero, once long ago, amid the turmoil of battle, the sounds of which grow fainter and fainter in his ears, as the colours of the world grow ever paler, while the body that only minutes ago was trembling now comes to rest, white as snow.

Lightning

In a large field cows were grazing, and when the rain came, five of them went over and stood beneath a big tree. Lightning struck the tree, the animals fell dead to the ground. I saw a photo of them in a newspaper, and for some reason or other it made such an impression on me, five big bodies scattered on the ground around a tree, that I still remember it. (It may also be that I never saw such a photo, but only read about the incident and turned it into an image in my memory.) People too are struck down every year by lightning, but it is the five cow carcasses I remember, maybe because the animals were unaware of the dangers of standing under a tree in a thunderstorm and didn't know what the brief flashes that at times lit up the sky might be, nor did they associate them with the thunder that rolled across the sky afterwards. The movements of lightning are mechanical, an immense light and an immense heat plunge down suddenly along channels in the sky, the forces thus released are tremendous, and while we, when a person is struck by lightning, think of this person as having been maximally unlucky, and thus have already located the incident within a human horizon, there is something about the animals' ignorance that turns the lightning strike into an event which is open, and which ties everything together: the green grassy field, the rain falling from the grey sky, the cows standing beneath the old oak tree, the thunder booming across the sky, the discharge of electricity that shoots down towards the tree, is conducted through it and out into the ground, up into the bodies, whose large hearts stop. The bang when lightning strikes, the silence afterwards. The rain that continues to fall upon the dead animals. That is what I thought about last night when lightning flashed and thunder roared outside. At first we sat in the living room, where we occasionally counted the seconds from the flash of lightning to the clap of thunder; the lightning was several kilometres away. The rain outside struck the ground so hard that the drops bounced back up again. The children brushed their teeth and went to bed, we read to them. After the lights were out, I lay in bed and read the news on my smartphone. Outside the whole sky lit up, and the thunderclap which came only seconds later was so loud it sounded as if the sky was being ripped apart. Mere seconds after that there was a tremendous boom, as if from an explosion. The whole house seemed to shake. I jumped up and stood in front of the window. Lightning must have struck right outside. But no houses or trees were on fire. Could it have struck the street? The children came in, they were frightened, and we stood together looking out on the empty road and the pouring rain. I felt shaky too, but mainly happy, in an intense way. They asked if it was dangerous, I said no, there were so many objects in the vicinity that were taller than the roof of our house. After a while they went back to bed. Before I fell asleep, it was the bang I thought about, how incredibly loud it had been. And about an evening in Malmö when we had stood on the terrace gazing out over the city, where the black, heavy sky split open in bolt after bolt of lightning, it seemed it would never end, and the sky that evening is surely the most beautiful thing I have seen. There are few sights I find more beautiful than that of lightning, and the sound of thunder always heightens the sense of being alive. Water and air, rain and clouds, they too have been here for ever, but they are such an integral part of life that their ancientness is never apparent in our thoughts or emotions, contrary to lightning and thunder, which only occur now and then, during brief intervals which we are at once familiar with and foreign to, just as we are at once familiar with and foreign to ourselves and the world we are a part of.

Chewing Gum

Chewing gum usually comes in two forms, either as small pillow-shaped pellets or as flat oblong sticks. The pellets have a fairly hard, smooth, enamel-like external layer, a kind of shell which makes a crunching sound when the teeth are pressed through it, and a softer gum centre which releases its strong taste as soon as the teeth reach it, not unlike the way a pharmaceutical capsule functions. These two different consistencies change rapidly once one begins to chew: in the first few seconds a porridge-like mass is formed, before what we think of as the real essence of gum emerges, firm and chewy, smooth and elastic. Chewing gum's second shape, the flat oblong stick, looks rather like a wide ribbon of fresh pasta, and its texture is very different from that of a pellet, since it lacks the candy shell and is therefore softer, nor does it have a gum centre where the taste is concentrated. What happens is that the stick sort of skips both the capsule phase, when the taste spurts into the surrounding mass, and the porridge phase, and goes straight to the intrinsic state of chewing gum.

From a purely physiological perspective, chewing something without swallowing is pointless. So is smoking, but when one smokes, stimulating and addictive substances are released, which explains why fully grown adults suck on cigarettes. Chewing gum does not produce any such effect and is perhaps most closely related to the dummies that infants suck on, where the reflex that this sets off first tricks the body into believing that it is working to get itself some food, then takes over entirely and turns sucking on something into an activity valuable in and of itself. It is obvious then that there is something infantile about chewing gum. I spend so much time by myself that it didn't even cross my mind when last week I drove over to a small fishing town about twenty kilometres away, to visit a German arts editor who lives there a few months of the year. I always chew gum while I'm writing and while I'm driving, and not just one or two of the little pellets, but whole packets at a time. By the time I parked the car outside the old captain's house where the editor stayed I had a huge wad of gum in my mouth. Not until I rang the bell and he opened the door did I remember it. I let it lie on one side of my mouth and tried hard not to chew on it while he showed me around the house. It was very beautiful, renovated and furnished in the modernist style, not a single object awry. I kept looking for a place to throw away the gum, but there wasn't one. We sat down, he served coffee, I discreetly removed the gum from my mouth and hid it in the palm of my hand. My index finger and thumb around the handle of the antique thin porcelain coffee cup, the other three fingers curled around the gum. We talked about literature, he told me about the two books he was working on. The gum no longer adhered only lightly to my skin, the protective layer of saliva was gone, so now it was stuck. I thought he would probably shake my hand when I took my leave of him and plucked up my courage. 'Do you have anywhere I can put this?' I asked finally. 'The gum?' he said. His facial expression and whole bearing in the second that followed, expressing partly surprise, partly reproof, maybe also contempt, is still engraved on my mind. *'Gum?'* he said. Then the moment had passed, and the wad of gum was now the most natural thing in the world. He tore off a piece of paper and handed it to me. 'There is a waste-paper basket beside the writing desk,' he said. Almost any other failing would have been met with indulgence, for I was there in my capacity as author, therefore artist, therefore someone who could cut off his own ear, someone who could spew out obscenities, someone who could be drunk, maybe even shoot up some heroin in his bathroom. For if substance abuse is foolish and infantile, it is also magnificent, at least in an artist, whose spirit rebels against conformity. Chewing gum was only transgressive when we were seven, eight years old, when chewing a small piece of gum with your mouth open was cool and having your mouth full gave you a certain status. I used to save mine, I remember. One wad of gum could last for several weeks back then. The taste was gone after a few hours, but not the texture. That is no longer the case. Since everything nowadays is sugar-free, the taste disappears after only a few minutes, and the consistency becomes loose and grainy, having lost its elastic quality entirely. With one exception: Juicy Fruit. In all the places I have lived and written, in Volda and Bergen, in Stockholm and Malmö, I knew which shops stocked Juicy Fruit. There were fewer and fewer of them, and I began to hoard the yellow packets. Even now my writing desk is always full of old wads of gum, which with their grey colour, hemispherical shape and many little indentations resemble shrunken brains. I can't write without them, and I don't discard them until the grainy phase sets in. Of the fortunate fact that I am not alone in suffering from this vice, unworthy in all its insignificance, I am reminded every time I'm in town, where pavements and squares outside the main public buildings are covered in white spots distributed as randomly as the stars in the sky, and in the darkness, lit up by street lamps and shimmering faintly against the black asphalt, what the gum-flecked pavements most resemble is indeed a starry sky.

Lime

Today there was a fog. The normally transparent and un-resisting air was hazy with moisture. Everything glistened, everything was still, and our white car stood gleaming on the gravel as I left the house to drive the children to school. The fog lay so densely that we couldn't see the fields we passed on the way. It was as if we were driving through a sea. I reflected that it didn't take more than a minor change in the weather such as this for the whole of logic to change. Fog obstructs vision and creates a different spatial dynamic. All of a sudden it is the small, everyday objects that come into view. The clear rainwater that had collected on the gravel in the ruts made by the wheels. The black car antenna, which I'd never noticed before. The shiny fuse box against the red wall of the house, half covered by climbing plants. This is how objects appear in dreams, where they are weighted by a different logic to that of the landscape. The dynamic of sounds was different too: our footsteps across the gravel seemed to stand alone, devoid of background; when I pressed the car door handle the click of metal sounded like a tiny explosion.

Now it is evening, and the fog has lifted. There is a wind blowing from the east, in from the sea, and it is laden with rain, pattering against the roof. It is as if a wall were standing open: the long, beautiful summer has ended, and everything rushes towards autumn. The leaves drop from the trees, the colours drift from green towards yellow and brown, the air smells of soil. It feels good. Whitewashing the house, which I intend to do tomorrow, also has a pleasurable side to it – it feels good in the same way that kindling a wood fire and getting the logs to catch feels good, or painting the wall of a house, as I did a few weeks ago.

Why is it good?

I don't know. When I'm in the middle of some practical task, there is nothing pleasurable about it, I just want to get it over with. So it must be the thought of work that pleases me. The thought of its manual aspect, its materiality. The wood, how it soaks up the paint and is then able to withstand rain and wind and snow for years afterwards. The colour, which is produced from substances extracted from a mine in the hills at Falun; they make the paint dry and somehow metallic, and cause it to rub off on the skin when one brushes the wood with one's hand. I get the same feeling from beer, which has always been brewed in the same way, of water, malt and hops, and from bread, especially when I bake it myself: knead the flour, the water, the salt and the yeast into a dough, wet and sticky at first, then slightly tacky, until it just barely clings to the skin, leave it to rise, roll out the loaves, put them in the oven, where they develop a hard, faintly burned surface and a soft dry inside. The basic, simple, fundamental aspect of it. Its tangibility and its ancientness: people have been doing this for thousands of years. In fact that whole reality is foreign to me, but whenever I've come into contact with it, I've enjoyed it. The feeling of being in the world and of being a part of it. To understand that when you touch something, you are actually touching something. Not just seeing, not just thinking, but grasping.

So I'm looking forward to whitewashing the house tomorrow, to moistening the wall thoroughly, brushing on the lime in thin layers so that the wall will absorb it, and to feeling myself lose control when water, rain and the soft lime-wash run together and drip all over the place, only to regain it tenfold later, when the work is done and the wall stands there gleaming, white and precise amid the grey. Or even better, amid the grey and green, like the wall at the edge of the garden last autumn. It wasn't just the wall that emerged from oblivion then, reasserting its rights, but that whole part of the garden, which suddenly came into view again, like when an old concept is inserted into a new context, and everything it once stood for again leaches into our thoughts about the world.

Adders

Adders can't hear, and that alone makes their world different from ours. It is true that they can perceive vibrations in the ground, which is a primitive form of hearing, but for us to be able to imagine what their existence is like as they glide across the forest floor, first of all we must subtract timbre and acoustics. There is no sound. No birdsong, no squawking of gulls, no rustle of leaves rising and falling as the wind surges through the trees, no whisper of water. And it's not like the adder knows that sounds actually exist but it just can't hear them. No, to the adder the wind that rushes through the woods on a stormy day is completely soundless, and the birds tilting their heads towards the sky and opening their beaks do so without a sound. The adder doesn't see very much either, its flat little head is always in close proximity to the ground so its reddish eyes see grass, heather, rock, soil strewn with pine needles, bared roots, but without taking notice of them, for what catches its attention are movements and scents. Its tongue, which it keeps flicking in and out, gathers scent molecules, which it reads and assigns meaning to, for if an animal has just passed, it leaves a trail of scent, which the adder can track. The world of the adder is soundless, overgrown, full of tremors and smells. It always knows if there are other adders nearby. In winter they seek out each other's company, as many as a hundred adders can hibernate together in burrows in the ground or under mounds of loose scree, where they lie motionless for months. When spring arrives, they are cold and move slowly and feebly. What that feels like, to wake up after having lain as if dead, without food or water, in a body that has been cold as ice and now slowly gets warmer, but not very much, only enough for them to rouse themselves, to feel that they exist, and wriggle out of their lair, is impossible to say. But they know about warmth and seek it. Slowly the adder slithers through its low, silent world towards an open, south-facing slope where the sun can warm it. If anyone comes trampling through the woods, which in our world might be equivalent to someone letting out a roar nearby, it glides into hiding and lies there perfectly still. Every single step of a boot travels through it. It's April, and though the sun is shining in the sky, the air is cold. The adder winds its way, emerges from the stunted woods onto the upper part of a pebble beach, a hundred metres or so above the sea, where it encounters a large slab of stone and remains there. A man and a boy come walking, and because of the pebbles, it doesn't notice them. The man stops, points out the adder to the boy, bends down and throws a rock, which strikes the adder's middle. It slinks away, is struck by another rock, and another. It writhes and wriggles as little by little it is covered in rocks. But there are spaces between the rocks, and it slithers through them. When the head pokes out from the pile, the man is standing only a yard away, and the stone that strikes its flat head crushes it.

More than forty years have passed since that happened.

I still wish he hadn't done it, and I still don't understand why he did, but he seemed to hate it more than any other thing. I had never seen him like that before, and never saw him like that again.

Mouth

The mouth is one of the five body orifices, and thus a site of exchange between the body and the world. The outermost part of the mouth is made up of the lips, two relatively long and narrow pads which lie horizontally against each other on the forward-facing side of the head, in the lower part of the face, below the nose. These pads are distinguished from all other visible parts of the body by being reddish, in contrast to the white, yellowish-white, brown or black skin stretched over the rest of the face, and by being moist. Both the moistness and the colour are characteristic of the interior of the body. This is so because the lips belong at once to the interior and to the exterior: they form the orifice. Such indeterminate zones, which are neither one thing nor the other, arise wherever the inner meets the outer, the wet meets the dry. In the body that is true of the anus, which like the lips is moist and has a different colour and texture to the surrounding skin, being faintly reddish-beige and slightly slimy. In nature a similar ambiguity is found in areas where water and land meet – on the foreshore, along riverbanks and in estuaries, where the ground is wet yet is neither a riverbed, a field nor meadow, but something in between, and this also characterises the forms of life found there, the fish-like creatures that roam as easily under water as above it. The lips and the anus are openings into the body's interior, but while the latter is a canal for the excretion of waste, closed by a muscle which opens in response to pressure from within, the lips are just the opposite, they protect an opening where matter from the outside is inserted into the body. Behind the lips, the teeth stand fence-like, hard and impervious, and behind this fence a grotto yawns, the mouth, the oral cavity. Its walls, the palate and the insides of the cheeks, are covered with a pale red mucous membrane, which is always wet, and from the centre of this grotto the tongue juts out, a large, mollusc-like muscle, also pale red, but in contrast to the hard palate soft, softer than the lips, however not smooth like them, but slightly rough. When the mouth is closed and the lips and the teeth are shut tight, the tongue fills nearly the entire oral cavity. It is attached to the floor of the mouth in much the same way as the fleshy interior of a mussel is attached to its shell. Above the root of the tongue is the opening to the throat, a tunnel which leads straight down into the depths of the body. From the roof of this tunnel hangs the uvula, a soft fleshy knob like a tiny stalactite, and behind it another narrow passage opens, this leads up to the nose and is thus directly connected to the outside world through the two nostrils, which in contrast to the mouth and the anus stand permanently open.

The mouth is where the sense of taste is located. This is where it is determined whether something tastes good or bad, sour or sweet, salt or bitter. The mouth is also the place where food is mashed together, work done by the teeth, assisted by the tongue, which pushes pieces of food in between the chomping gums, the first step in the process of digestion, the objective being to transform as much as possible of this extrinsic matter into something intrinsic. This labour is accompanied by many pleasurable sensations, such as the slightly bitter taste that fills the mouth when a juicy lettuce leaf meets the tongue, and the wonderful feeling of crispiness that follows when the teeth crunch through its fresh, firm surface. There is no reason to think that other kinds of mouths, such as those found in rabbits or guinea pigs, partake of this feast with any less pleasure than ours. The fact that all animals have mouths and can hardly be conceived of without them – as opposed to ears or eyes, for example – alone forces one to admit that Aristotle is right when he writes that everything that lives has a soul, but perhaps also to add that everything that lives experiences pleasure, or at least satisfaction that something tastes good when the mouth is opened and something from the outside is inserted into it and ground together while little bursts of taste flash through the head and the nagging feeling of hunger slowly fades away.

Daguerrotype

The photograph is associated with modernity and with things mechanical, it belongs to our technological age and is part of what makes our culture different from those that preceded it. But the principle that certain substances are sensitive to light and that light can imprint itself on them was known at least as early as the Middle Ages, by Albertus Magnus for instance, Thomas Aquinas's teacher. He was a theologian and a philosopher, and was canonised after his death. He was also rumoured to have been an alchemist. There is something captivating about the thought that he or another Aristotelian of the Middle Ages or the Renaissance might have stood in his study, surrounded by liquids and substances, experimenting with silver nitrate, mercury, copper and glass, and suddenly one day have succeeded in fixing light to a plate, so that the room he was standing in appeared in negative. Technically it would not have been impossible, since all the necessary substances and materials existed then as now. But that these might be used to reproduce the world lay so far beyond their conceptual horizon, their notions about the nature of the world and what it meant to be a human being, that it could not be thought. And yet in a sense this is where photography began, not through the insight that light could imprint itself on silver nitrate, but through the slow turn of thought towards the material world that the philosophy of nature represented. In the 1820s it was no longer unthinkable, and a number of people were experimenting with light-sensitive substances, among them Joseph Niépce, whose image of Burgundy, taken in 1826 or 1827, is considered the oldest surviving photograph. It consists of a few darker and lighter areas on a metal plate, and is so blurred that it takes a while to real-ise that the dark areas are the walls and roofs of buildings, the light area the sky. Niépce took the photograph from an attic window, the image fixed on the plate is the view from his window that day. That there is something ghostly about all photographs from this early period is due not merely to the haziness and indistinctness of their subject matter, which seems almost to hover, as if the material objects depicted belonged to another dimension, but also because they don't portray people. The exposure time was several hours, so that only unmoving objects were fixed to the plate. That is perhaps the most incredible thing about these early photographs, that they relate to time in such a way that only the most lasting of appearances are visible and the human form is shown to be so fleeting and ephemeral that it leaves no trace anywhere. To creatures whose experience of time is slower than ours, this is how the world would appear. Such an outside per-spective was not unthinkable, for the divine, the Lord God and his angels, whose existence people still believed in, were changeless and stood outside time. As they gazed upon the world, human affairs must have seemed so hasty and short-lived that they didn't register. The very first photograph of a human being was taken by Louis Daguerre eleven or twelve years after Niépce captured the view from his window. This too was from a window, overlooking the Boulevard du Temple one morning in 1838, and with such a long exposure time that only the unmoving was fixed in the image. The street is flooded in sunlight, a row of trees casts long shadows across the pavement, and every detail, from the many chimneys and roof ridges to the window sashes in the nearest, white apartment building, stands out sharp and clear. It is an unsettling image, for judging by the time of day there ought to be plenty of people, horses and carriages outside. But there are only two. In the lower left part of the picture, where a sunlit pavement begins and just where the photo is divided in the golden ratio, a man stands with one leg lifted. Ever since I saw this photograph for the first time, I have felt it to be a picture of the Devil. As the only person to show up clearly in what was in fact a bustling street, he had a durability and a permanence that allowed his image to be fixed onto the daguerrotype. Something about the figure makes me think that the very next moment he must have turned his head and glanced up at the photographer. But the photographer never saw what the photograph depicts. Louis Daguerre saw a teeming city street, and possibly didn't even notice this man until hours later when the photograph was developed, and all the others, except this one figure, were gone.

Letter to an Unborn Daughter

29 September. The day began as usual, I got your sisters and brother out of bed, made breakfast for them and took them to the school bus, then I worked a little before we got into the car and drove to Ystad. We were going to see the midwife. Even though we have been through all the phases of this nine-month-long process thrice, there is still a touch of solemnity about a visit like this. Linda sat next to me in the passenger seat with the safety belt strapped across her belly. I thought of you, that you were in there, and that I had to drive carefully. The midwife's office was in a small building outside the town centre, near all the shopping malls. The day was grey and the surroundings cheerless as we left the car in the large parking area outside, but all that was forgotten when our turn came up and we entered the examination room, for we were there to see you. After a brief conversation the midwife asked Linda to lie on the couch. I sat down next to her. The midwife pulled up Linda's sweater and bared her belly, then put some transparent jelly on it, moved the little probe over the skin, and on the screen across the room your body emerged, surrounded by dark liquids and close walls. The image, with all its grainy zones and shadowy, almost dreamlike movements, looked as though it was being transmitted from a place far, far away,

in outer space or down in the depths of the ocean, and it was impossible to connect the image with either the humdrum room we were sitting in or with Linda's faintly bulging stomach, even though I knew that that was where it came from. In a sense the feeling I had of enormous distance was accurate, for the prenatal state, the body growing inside a hollow filled with liquids within the mother's body, and there apparently repeating every developmental stage that the human being has undergone, is connected to the primordial, and is separated from us by an abyss, not in space but in time. And yet modern technology is what makes this image possible. And then the being we were watching was you. It was you moving your limbs so slowly, not a lizard or a turtle. We saw your heart, it was beating fast the way it was supposed to and had all the chambers it should have. We saw your face, the little nose, and we saw the brain, small but complete. We saw the spine, the hands, the fingers, the shin bone, the thigh bone. You lay with your legs pulled up to your chest, and you kept moving one of your hands, which seemed to float off on its own, opening, closing. They told us that in all probability you are a girl.

So you are Anne.

The parents give the child life, the child gives the parents hope. That is the transaction.

Does that sound like a burden?

It isn't. Hope makes no demands.

And I am sentimental. But how to write about this, which is so small and so great, so simple and so complicated, so trivial and so...well, sacred?

Sentimental is another word for emotional. But what are

emotions? What do we feel when we feel? We call sentimental that which exaggerates feeling, which wastes it. So does that make level-headedness the highest value?

The stars are out tonight. I was just outside taking a leak on the lawn, something I do only when everyone is asleep and I'm alone. Day after day of open, clear skies, that is how the summer has been from May up until now, sun during the day, stars at night. Nothing is finer than the ebb of a good summer, it has left behind a sort of satiation, something has been filled, and now it turns, now the village is no longer surrounded by gently waving fields quite indescribably golden beneath the high blue sky – seen from the road the ripe fields resemble lakes between the clustered houses – but stubble fields, for in the past few weeks combine harvesters and tractors have been gliding slowly back and forth across them, and tall rows of compressed hay bales have been left behind here and there, like high walls against the wind, which now comes blowing in from the Baltic Sea with increasing frequency.

Something has been filled, now it is emptying: the air of warmth, the trees of fruit and leaves, the fields of grain. And all the while you are growing silently in the darkness.

OCTOBER

Fever

I have a fever. I feel cold even though my body temperature is a couple of degrees higher than normal. My skin is also more sensitive than usual; every touch feels uncomfortable, even the slight pressure of clothing. This makes it clear to me how well adapted the body normally is to the world, how it merges with it as if the world were transmitting at a certain frequency and the body were exactly tuned to receive it. Within that zone, where the body's frequency is identical to the world's, whatever happens meets with no resistance. The body walks about in the world, is enveloped in its air, touches its objects and surfaces, and even if these should be as different from one another as the soft, moist flannel that one hand is squeezing and the hard edge of the bath that the other hand is supporting itself against, both are within the spectrum that we are open to, so that they almost escape us entirely, in the never formulated yet constant sensation that the world is an extension of the body. When a fever comes on, sensitivity increases, and the body is somehow lifted out of its intimacy with the world, which suddenly presses in on all sides and becomes noticeable, not outright hostile, but alien. But not only does fever enter into horizontal liaisons with the objects surrounding it, it also opens a vertical axis, cutting down into the past, since by virtue of being an exceptional state it also awakens the memory of its earlier manifestations. This is why fever also always has a good side. I write this at my desk in a small house in Glemmingebro, near the southernmost tip of Sweden, in every way far removed from the place where I grew up and the person I was then. And yet that world has been strangely present ever since I got out of bed a few hours ago. New recollections keep emerging into consciousness. Perception of time changed while the fever lasted, suddenly I could be wide awake in a perfectly silent house surrounded by darkness, as if night were a beach I had washed up on. But more important, and this is the good part of having a fever, was the care I received. *Are you feeling warm?* And after the question came the hand touching my brow. *You're running a fever!* With fever came privileges. Meals in bed. Grapes. New comic books. With fever came attention. Continual questions about how I was doing, how I felt. The hand brushing against my forehead, the fingers running through my hair. Ordinarily no one ever touched me, caresses were rare in our family, except if one was ill and running a fever, and the resulting paradoxical sensation is something I still remember, how uncomfortable these touches felt on my febrile skin, and how comforting they felt to me.

Rubber Boots

Since rubber boots are shaped to fit the foot and the upper calf, sort of like a sheath, when they are standing unused on the floor in the hall they can at first glance look like an actual foot and lower leg, seemingly amputated just below the knee. This is something they have in common with hanging jackets and shirts, which can also resemble the bodies they sheathe. When I enter the hall in the late evening or early morning, it is as if impressions of the entire family's bodies are hanging on pegs and standing on the floor in the dark, like their negatives as it were. Then the thought may come to me of what life would be like had they died in an accident and all that was left were the spaces they once occupied. With my rubber boots this is in fact the case, since I inherited them from my father when he died. The space that his feet and lower legs once filled is now standing on the floor by the wall in the hall. I no longer think of him very often, but I do every time I stick my feet into my boots, which fit me like a glove, and walk around in the garden in them. Of all the things he left behind, I took only two, his binoculars and his rubber boots. Why just those two I don't know. Perhaps because they were neutral and yet useful at the same time? I could never have taken nor worn his lambskin jacket, for instance, it was too close to him, too typical an expression of him, I could never have shouldered it, nor wanted to, while rubber boots are not in any comparable way an expression of individuality, but are more or less the same for everyone. Nor could I have taken the paintings he had on his walls, they were close to him in a similar way, since he had selected just those pictures and had taken pleasure in looking at them and owning them, while the binoculars do not partake of this individuality, they're just binoculars, made to magnify whatever is far away, just as the boots are made to keep water out. Which they are perfect for. The surface of the thick, rather stiff rubber is shiny and smooth, so that water cannot cling to it, there are no cracks or tears it can penetrate; instead it glides slowly down to the ground or forms a moist and almost imperceptible membrane around the rubber, while the leg fits so snugly around the calf that the opening into the boot's interior is sealed. That the boot is absolute proof against weather can occasion great pleasure – just think of the feeling one gets when one goes walking across a muddy field and the foot sinks down into the mud without anything penetrating its protective cover, the mud oozes up around the boot but the foot remains dry – and sovereign, somehow. For isn't the feeling of sovereignty the very cause of the joy one may feel walking through a marsh or maybe wading in a brook in heavy waterproof boots? To be invulnerable, to be protected, to be a separate entity in the world? Yes, oh yes, that is *precisely* wherein joy over the properties of the boots lies.

Jellyfish

Whereas one can still somehow relate to primitive creatures like sharks, crocodiles and ostriches, in the sense that they have eyes and can see, and a brain, though a small one, so that they can act on the basis of emotions like desire or fear, jellyfish are such primitive and simple organisms that it is impossible to identify with them. Nothing of what characterises our lives can be found in the existence they lead. But although jellyfish appeared on earth six hundred million years ago and were the first beings to evolve from a single cell to a creature consisting of multiple cells, they are also our contemporaries. What we call life, to be alive, is a grace they too partake of. In appearance jellyfish resemble bells, with long veils trailing behind them. Some of them are almost entirely transparent, these are called moon or saucer jellies. Some are orange or blue, these are stinging jellyfish. They live in the ocean and have a strange, almost majestic air of dignity about them as they float through the water. They can propel themselves forward by contracting and then dilating their bodies, like a slowly pumping muscle, but their power of movement is infinitely small compared to the might of ocean streams, so their eventual destination is beyond their control. These bells of the ocean are blind and mute but not insensate, for while they lack a brain, nerve threads run through their bodies, and while they may not feel hunger or desire such as we understand them, they do eat and reproduce. When we contemplate the meaning of life, it is towards the jellyfish or the fungi, both of which were among the earliest multicellular organisms on the planet, that we must turn. What do they live for? In what does their life consist? And perhaps most importantly, what is it worth? When I was growing up, moon jellies were things we scooped up out of the sea and threw at each other, like snowballs, they fitted so snugly in the hand and made such horrid slapping noises when they struck someone's back or thigh. Stinging jellyfish were creatures we were always on the lookout for when we went swimming, everyone had at one time or another been stung by their long, invisible tentacles, and everyone had felt the pain, which was worse than that of nettles maybe because the sting of jellyfish often affected large areas of the skin if one had got all tangled up in them. The stinging jellyfish looked like little suns as they drifted through the water, from their circular orange bodies to the rays that shot out of them. Their strangeness – that they were unlike anything else we knew of – never occurred to us. They were a part of the world, like moss or seaweed, grass or fire. Not until I was eleven years old, walking with my father along the smooth stone slopes at the far end of the island where we lived, did I glimpse the fantastical thing about them. We had reached the edge of the cliff, and in the sea below us, a drop of maybe seven metres, several hundred jellyfish were gathered together, swaying like flotsam in the waves that swept into this little backwater of the universe.

I often drive the children into Ystad to school, and on the way we pass an artillery range several kilometres long. It lies by the sea and encompasses the beaches, the fields and the long green hills that rise up towards the edge of the cliffs, from which one can see for miles around. This morning the flag on the cliffs had been hoisted, a signal that the military were conducting firing exercises. Though we live five kilometres from the range, at times we can hear the booming, a strange, dreamlike, almost hypnotic sound. Russia is rearming, military activity at the borders is increasing, which has led to public debate about the reduction of Sweden's defence capabilities over the past few decades. Yet the thought of war in this beautiful landscape remains remote, as dreamlike as the muffled but thunderous roar of the guns that I can hear in the afternoons as I rake up fallen leaves in the garden. What war entails I don't know, but I imagine that I am sometimes able to grasp certain aspects of it, as when I read an article a few weeks ago about deaths in motor racing, which said that there was no culture of safety in the decade following the Second World War because people were used to the thought that human beings could die, it seemed almost acceptable to them. This appears a reasonable and a probable theory, yet it shocked me since I could relate it to our own time and in that way catch sight of one of the consequences of war. Since war is a state of emergency, a zone within human society in which ordeals and atrocities occur but which most of us view from the outside almost in the same way that we respond to atrocities in fiction, it touches only our rational side, that part of us which understands and condemns, or alternatively understands and accepts. The nature of war, however, is precisely to tear rationality asunder, to break down all rules, laws and agreements, to destroy all established values and in that way penetrate to our innermost beliefs, those that concern who we are. I can't think of a single war that hasn't been about identity. And identity is so fundamental to our being, so closely linked to our emotions and drives and so far beyond the reach of reason that it can neither be thought up or thought away; whatever war tears asunder, its consequences, remain unapprehended by all except those who take part in it.

In Sweden, where I live, war has not been waged since the seventeenth century, that is since the time of Montaigne, Cervantes and Shakespeare. This does not mean that war is a thing of the past, for it is ever-present in culture; hardly an evening goes by without a soldier appearing on TV, hardly a day passes without the newspapers mentioning war. There is a boy in our neighbourhood who is nine years old and who is always playing war games. For him any situation can become a combat situation. At home he has a whole arsenal of weapons. Swords and bucklers, bows and arrows, crossbows, pistols, revolvers, rifles, automatic rifles, big futuristic make-believe weapons made of plastic. Together with his father he watches movies from the Second World War, long black-and-white sequences from the Pacific with

Japanese planes being shot down by American naval vessels or plummeting down and crashing into them, submarines torpedoing ships, sequences from continental Europe with soldiers crawling across snow or mud and the lightning fire of Katyusha multiple rocket launchers, nicknamed Stalin's organs by German troops. One time I knocked on their door I found him lying on the floor with a helmet on his head, a gun in his hand and both his parents busy bandaging him with toilet paper. He was playing wounded soldier.

Why he is constantly going to war, young as he is, I obviously don't know. But it might be because war games are the only thing he knows of that deflect aggression, that don't shut it in but allow it to flow out, not freely and unrestrainedly and causing anxiety, but along definite channels and corridors in his world. For that is the other side of war: it simplifies life, sets up concrete objectives and assigns to each and every one definite tasks which can be solved by applying clear-cut methods. War unleashes not only the irrational forces latent in humans, but also the rational. War is both the simple shape of the arrowhead and the complicated life that it annihilates. The simple and hard help the boy next door to bring order to the complex and soft, and the booms he will hear when he gets home from school today will fill him with joy, for they hold a promise of something even simpler and harder, the allure of which we have all experienced.

Labia

Labia is the name given to the oblong folds that, from either side, meet above the urethral orifice and the vaginal opening in women, and cover these openings like a curtain of skin. There are two pairs of labia, the outer and the inner. In infants the skin is smooth and even, and the faintly rounded fissure created by the two slightly chubby, almost pillow-like parts has a shape and a size that bring to mind a coin slot or a small mouth. When an infant girl is lying on the changing table, she might at times put her hand into the fissure, uncovering the faintly reddish, moistly glistening parts within. A father may only wash this part of the female body while the child is very young, at least that is what I did; as soon as my girls were old enough, I handed them a flannel lathered with soap and asked them to wash themselves while they sat in the tub. This was because in recent decades the male gaze has become suspect, and the vague but constant guilt this arouses penetrated all the way into the relationship between father and child, which when it came to nudity was characterised by exaggerated caution. Indeed, guilt has penetrated even as far as this text, for isn't the comparison with a coin slot inappropriately objectifying and essentially misogynistic? But a body is always also simply a body, anatomy, biology, and is decoded as such the first time it becomes visible to the world, during the ultrasound examination, when fingers and toes are counted, bone lengths and skull diameter are measured, heart function is checked and sex is determined. That certain organs of the body are concealed later in life, and cannot even be mentioned or described without arousing shame, is perhaps the most characteristically human thing of all. Shame is like a lock, it shuts away what must be shut away, and is one of the most important mechanisms of social life. Shame regulates differences, creates secrets, builds up a charge. The counterforce and antithesis of shame is desire, which with all its being seeks to eliminate differences, to do away with secrets, release tensions. The main battle between shame and desire is waged over sexuality. One of the most interesting things about these two notions is that they are akin to fiction, in the sense that both of them deal with alternative realities. Shame relates to reality as it ought to be, not reality as it is. Desire for its part transcends material reality and transforms it into its own images, which, while desire persists, appear immensely pleasurable, but which resume their more neutral forms as soon as desire wanes. To me, these three levels of reality are joined in the female external genitalia, with their double set of lips which in earlier times went by the Latin name of pudenda, which literally means 'things to be ashamed of'. For into these faintly urine-scented folds, wrinkled as elephant hide but infinitely softer, I often feel a wild longing to stick my tongue. When they are moistened by secretions so that they seem almost liquefied, the longing expands into wanting to press my whole face against them, to let my nose slide in between those lips of shame, to suckle, suck and lick them. Now, as I write this, such behaviour feels entirely alien to me, and undesirable, for urine and excrement and the channels transporting them are normally something I prefer to keep away both from my thoughts and from my face. And I am glad I have never seen myself from the outside in this situation, for what must I look like, if not an animal wildly slurping something down? But as soon as coitus has been consummated and we lie on our backs in bed gazing up at the ceiling or at each other, it is as if we have returned from a journey. We cover ourselves and turn once more to each other's faces, the comforting familiarity of the eyes, the mirrors of the soul, the inner person's unique light, and once again it becomes possible to consider the union of man and woman as something exalted and sacred.

Beds

With its four legs and its flat, soft surface, the bed gently accommodates one of our most basic needs: it is good to lie down in bed, and it is good to sleep there through the night. The bed is placed in the bedroom, which is often the innermost room in the house or apartment, and in two-storey houses the bedroom is usually on the upper floor. This is so because we are never as vulnerable as when we are asleep, we lie defenceless in our beds at night without knowing what is going on around us, and to withdraw from sight at such a time, to conceal ourselves from other animals and human beings, is an instinct that runs deep in us. The bed is also a place we retreat to in order to get some peace, since with most people sleep requires quiet and seclusion. So the bed, then, is a kind of hiding place, but inasmuch as everyone has one, not one associated with secrecy but rather with a sort of discretion. Just how fundamental the bed, the bedroom and sleep are to our lives is not something we usually give much thought to, since they are saturated with lifelong habit and are always associated precisely with discretion. But if it were possible to see everyone who has retired to their beds in a great city at night, in London, New York or Tokyo, for example, if we imagined that the buildings were made of glass and that all the rooms were lit, the sight would be deeply unsettling. Everywhere there would be people lying motionless in their cocoons, in room after room for miles on end, and not just at street level, along roads and crossroads, but even up in the air, separated by plateaus, some of them twenty metres above ground, some fifty, some a hundred. We would be able to see millions of immobile people who have withdrawn from others in order to lie in a coma throughout the night. Sleep's vertiginous link to primordial times, not just with human life as it first unfolded on the plains of Africa three hundred thousand years ago, but with life on earth in its very first form, rising out of the sea and coming ashore four hundred million years ago, would become apparent. And a bed would no longer be merely a piece of furniture acquired from a shop, but a boat that every human being has and which we board every evening to let ourselves be carried through the night.

Fingers

As I write this, Linda and Christina are sitting outside drinking coffee at the table set against the wall of the house across
the lawn, maybe twelve metres away. It is a chilly morning,
they are wearing heavy jackets, the only parts of them that are
bare are their faces and hands. One moment they exchange
familiar glances and smile, the next their glances part, and
their hands reach for their coffee cups, which they raise to
their mouths and sip before setting them down again on the
little wrought-iron table. Christina yawns, Linda lifts her hand
to the side of her face as if to shield it from the glare of the low,
cold sun, and at the same time she says something. I don't
know what she is saying, but I can see her lips moving and
then Christina nodding. She has a hand on each knee, her
fingers are spread out, the blue material of her trousers visible between them. Linda and I have been together for eleven
years, and I have known Christina for just as long. When I
look at them, it seems my gaze always takes as its starting
point the person each one is to me, an integrated whole, an
unquestioned entity (but not unchangeable), and from there
proceeds to the details, such as the face and the eyes, the
hands, the fingers. That they are Linda's or Christina's fingers
is never absent from my mind, they are almost synecdochic,

parts which for the moment represent the whole. If it were not so, we would see every human being as a cacophony of body parts, organs and movements, producing an endless stream of disparate moods, phrases and expressions, and would go about in a state of permanent confusion. We understand ourselves in a similar fashion, we posit a similar entity as regards who we are, yet there is still a major difference, in that the entity in which we, as it were, encapsulate other people, is not an external entity, but rather an inner one. Others, then, exist *inside* us, side by side with the person we are to ourselves, and since anything like partitions or walls is foreign to the world of thought and emotion, it is not unreasonable to imagine that all these various entities – which include not only people, but trees, tables, bicycles, houses, plains, lakes, cats, cups, telephones and electric torches, to take only those examples that sprang to my mind first – are also parts of our personality, are also parts of who we are and stand in a similar relation to identity as Christina's fingers for me stand in relation to Christina's person.

With my own fingers it is a different matter. When I look at them, there is no way I can connect them with who I am. When I crook them towards my palms and turn them face up, I see four brothers who resemble each other and who stick together against their father, who is always at a certain distance from them, thicker, stronger. Their faces, which are the nails, are smooth as windowpanes and therefore hold out the promise that one can see through them, which one can't, their grey-white colour is impenetrable: they look like blind people.

If I turn my hand over and stretch my fingers out, they resemble worms or little snakes, the nails being their heads, each setting out in its own direction.

When the children were small I often let two of my fingers amble towards them, stop, lift one foot and bend it as if in greeting while I said *Hello, hello* in a squeaky voice. I named this creature the Fingerman. To them it was magic, the fingers' connection to me ceased the moment they began to walk and seemed to become a separate entity, an autonomous being out walking on the table who stopped to greet them. They liked it, they smiled, and when the Fingerman ran towards them, leaped across the cleft separating the table from their chair, landed on their bellies and ran up their necks to tickle them, they laughed with delight.

Now, on the rare occasions when I trot him out again, one of my daughters becomes uneasy. She is nearly a teenager, and as tough and as vulnerable as only children of that age can be. If she sees the Fingerman rise to his feet on the table and start walking towards her, she says, *Don't, Daddy. Don't do it.* If I carry on, she stands up and says, *I don't want to.* She laughs as she says it, for she knows it's silly and childish, but she is also genuinely unsettled, I can see it in her eyes and hear it in her voice. This is so, I think, because the question of who she is has begun to trouble her for the first time, and with it, the question of who we are, her parents and her family. The Fingerman transforms me into body parts, and the body parts into autonomous beings, and since one of the many possible truths about reality is that it is essentially non-attached and turned away like a blind eye, the game opens an abyss. The other children are too young to feel threatened by it, I am too old. This chasm at the centre of the world opens only to one who is neither child nor adult, but midway between.

Autumn Leaves

The leaves of the chestnut tree have begun to fall onto the flagstone path in the garden, which is visible only here and there. The willow too has lost its leaves and needs pruning, it grows monstrously fast. The apple tree's foliage has also thinned out, but from its boughs there are apples hanging, resembling little red lanterns amid all the naked branches. I ate one today, they are large, more red than green, and juicy, perhaps a little too sour, maybe they ought to be left for another week. I walked across the grass, long, soft and green, with the tart taste in my mouth, and thought about taste, the tastes of the various apple varieties, how old these tastes might be. When were they first crossbred? During the nineteenth century? The twentieth? Some tastes found in the world today are identical to tastes that existed two thousand years ago. The slightly unusual aroma, the out-of-the-ordinariness one can encounter in an apple from a private garden give me pleasure. I often think of my grandmother then, my father's mother, the apples from their garden which we got every autumn, sometimes a whole crate, which lay in our cellar for weeks. Yes, and the smell in their cellar, of apples and plums. She was interested in everything to do with plants and gardening. Her son, my father, shared this interest. Yet I don't feel any sense of continuity when I think of them in this way, they are strangers to me. And that feels good. It feels like I have started something new, something quite different, and that is this family. I think of it every day, that what matters is now, that the years we are living through now are when everything important happens. My previous life seems more and more distant. I am no longer preoccupied with my own childhood. Not interested in my student years, my twenties. All that seems far, far away. And I can imagine how it will be when what is happening now is over, when the children have moved out, the thought that these were the important years, this is when I was alive. Why didn't I appreciate it while I had it? Because then, I sometimes think, I hadn't had it yet. Only what slips through one's fingers, only what is never expressed in words, has no thoughts, exists completely. That is the price of proximity: you don't see it. Don't know that it's there. Then it is over, then you see it.

The yellow-red leaves lying wet and smooth on the flagstones between the houses. How the stone darkens when it rains, lightens as it dries.

Bottles

Though the bottle's basic form is always the same, a smooth cylinder-shaped body which narrows into a neck, its physiognomy is surprisingly multifarious. Between the squat short-necked bottle and the slender long-necked one there are infinite varieties. Bottles are made to store liquids, mainly those that we drink – the liquids we don't drink, such as perfume, petrol, paint, are generally stored in flasks, drums and cans – and as is the case with most forms, the shape of a bottle is almost entirely eclipsed by its contents, which is what we see, think of and associate with it: wine, beer, spirits, soft drinks. That the bottle itself is almost wholly invisible, that our thoughts, which follow our gaze, hardly ever fasten on it, is striking, since after all the bottle always determines how we view its contents. Few things are more undifferentiated than liquids, and no one can distinguish between beers when they are kept in large vats or barrels; it is only when it is bottled that beer gains its identity and becomes what we think of when we see it, while the thing that conveys this identity, the bottle, its distinctive form and colour, disappears. In literature this phenomenon is held up as an ideal: the form should shape the text but not be conspicuous in itself, what matters are the emotions and thoughts it evokes, while the text itself, to those who discern it, should be as cold and clear as glass. Another essential feature of bottles is that they are mass-produced. They are stacked on pallets and distributed from production plants via sales points to the individual household, where they are so common that a house without them is hardly imaginable. When I was little I thought of bottles as brothers, and if one bottle was standing by itself on the table, the large brown one-litre bottle from Arendal Brewery, for instance, with its characteristic yellow label depicting a ship in full sail stuck on the side, I felt sorry for it, while conversely I felt happy on the occasions when it stood there together with two or three of its jolly brothers or in a crate down in the cellar with the whole lot of them, as if asleep. But though the bottles were identical, they meant different things. At home on the living-room table they stood for joy, they meant that daddy was indulging himself a little, while outside, in the hands of youths they were synonymous with the forbidden and the wicked, or in the hands of grown-ups with alcoholism, which was terrible, though I didn't know exactly why, except that it entailed a drastic loss of dignity. There was only one drunkard in the neighbourhood where I grew up, he lived in one of the houses that were there before the housing development appeared, and we knew nothing about him apart from that. Once when he was pushing his bicycle up the hill with two white plastic bags dangling from the handlebars, I ran up to him, incited by my playmates. In a flash I lifted the plastic handles aside and peered into one of the bags. *It's full of beers!* I shouted and ran away as fast as I could. *He's got beer in his bag!* The others shouted, *Egge is a drunk*, while he climbed heavily onto the bicycle and continued on his way with the handlebars wavering because of the bags. I can still recall the feeling I had as I shouted to the others, for there wasn't any beer in the bags, only bread and milk, the safety that lay in the thought that the truth didn't matter, that about him I could lie since he was nothing but a drunk.

Stubble Fields

Why is it that we aren't more expectant than we are when we turn a corner in a city? After all, anything may await us there. Witold Gombrowicz expresses his bafflement at this in his diary. The uncertain and the unsure, all that we know nothing about, belong not only to metaphysics, concern not only the big questions about whether God exists or what awaits us after death, but also perfectly commonplace matters. Now Gombrowicz didn't have children, and even if he had, it isn't certain that would have influenced his view of the world or his thoughts about how it is taken for granted, but for me, reading Gombrowicz's diary as a childless person and then as the father of children have been two different experiences, since the main thing in the upbringing of children or in living with children is precisely to ensure that they get the feeling that the world is predictable, that it is graspable and at all times recognisable. To a child, the worst thing is not knowing what is going to happen, or indeed when it gets the feeling that anything at all can happen. That's why the child cries when a masked Santa Claus appears in the family's midst on Christmas Eve. Dread of the unknown or the unpredictable lies at our very core, obviously because it could once have been life-threatening, and it is countered by an equally fundamental effort to neutralise the unknown. The infant is calmed by repetition, the twelve-year-old depends on something remaining the same when the outside world opens up uncontrollably. So when the forty-year-old turns the corner of a building, the conviction that everything will be just as expected is so deeply rooted in him that it has become the very nature of reality, not just his conception of it.

When the Norwegian poet Olav H. Hauge wrote that it's possible to live in the everyday as well, he must have been thinking of this. But he did so with resignation, for although the fantastic for him was associated with madness and had as its consequence the straitjacket, involuntary medication and the eventless routines of the mental institution, sometimes in the form of stays that lasted for years, still the fantastic was of great value since it produced not just a feeling but a certainty that another level of reality existed, which entailed a whole other intensity of living.

This, which must be one of the forms that ecstasy takes, to me is merely theory. Reading Hauge's early poems, I imagine that they were a reined-in form of ecstasy, a way of grounding it, whereas his final poems, which in his diary he somewhat scornfully referred to as cold forging, have no contact at all with that dimension. Indeed, while in his early poems he sought to lessen the impact of ecstasy, which came from above, in his final poems he sought to invoke it from below with the means at his disposal there, birds and apples, snow and axes. Without success; the objects and the animals remained in the realm of the tangible, albeit not exactly the same as before, for after being touched by Hauge's gaze and words, they glow faintly.

Here but no further, I think as I drive the children to and from school and see the pale brown stubble in the fields along the road, for exceptionally it too seems to glow faintly when the fire-yellow light of the low autumn sun shines on it. But usually it is the other way round, the stubble appears to absorb the light, as does the entire landscape here in autumn, lying pale and waterlogged beneath the colourless, weakly lit sky. Even when the landscape contracts, the way it does when the manifold events occurring in it all point in the same direction – wind blows, rain flies through the air, car drives up the hill, to the left stubble, to the right soil, the sky blue-grey, the light scant, the view towards the sea closed off by fog, driver leans forward to see better through the windscreen trembling with rain and a falcon bursts suddenly across his field of vision, its large wings outstretched – the landscape is still nothing other than itself, and the sensation the driver may have, of a few seconds of dizzying intensity of being, is not the result of anything opening up, but its opposite, of something becoming denser. The ensuing sorrow, that this is all there is, is what Gombrowicz, who hated all notions of the high and sublime, dissolves in his speculations about the small and insignificant.

Badgers

One would think that the badger, with its characteristic snout, which is white and black and resembles nothing else in the fauna of the Nordic countries, and its broad, somehow flat body would be remarkable enough that stories would be told about it. One would think that seeing a badger would be something significant. But that is not the case. While the bear, the fox and the wolf all have prominent places in folk mythology, the badger is hardly mentioned. Accordingly it is not assigned human qualities in the way the others are, it is neither genial, nor clever, nor gullible, nor wicked, instead there is something vague and evasive about it. What is the badger really like? In appearance it is a little like the pine marten, and it is a little like the bear in that it hibernates in winter. It lives in clans of ten to fifteen members, typically in dense forest, often in the vicinity of open fields, where it gets its food at night. The badger is closely associated with the earth; it digs networks of burrows underground, which sometimes remain in use for several hundred years. There it sleeps during the day and throughout the winter. It also finds much of its food in the soil, eating earthworms in particular. That the badger has not been subsumed into culture enables us to see what culture does to the other animals which we have some kind of hold over, which we are familiar with and use to populate the stories we tell our children. The badger has existed outside all this, as if it has been a protected species, and when it stands at the edge of the woods looking at us, without us knowing, its gaze is that of all wild animals, attentive, alert, cogitating in a way that we don't understand, entirely in its own right. Its world is that of the low. It is the forest floor, which its broad body almost brushes against as it moves along, and it is the soil, which it burrows its paws and snout into, and wriggles down through in tunnels to sleep for several months during winter. Filled with the dark scents of the earth it must be. I myself have only seen a badger a handful of times, always in the same place, outside the house where I lived as a teenager – the house stood at the edge of the woods, with a view of a field and a river, perfect terrain for badgers. The woods were mixed forest, dense and difficult to penetrate, and down through the trees, maybe twenty metres from the house, a brook ran towards the river. I used to walk up along the brook from the road, it was a short cut. One evening when I was on my way home, it was summer and the sky was light, a badger came lumbering along the road. I had heard that badgers could bite through bone, and jumped up on the kerbstone with my heart beating fast. It stopped and stared at me, clearly evaluating the situation, whether it could get past me. It couldn't, so it turned and lumbered back the same way, then disappeared up along the course of the brook. That summer I was working at a local radio station and took the bus to and from town, so I passed the same place at the same hour several times a week. The badger clearly had fixed habits too, for I met it several times, assuming it was the same one. Sometimes I would hear it come rustling down along the brook, then I would run back to the road and walk on a little way so as not to block the badger's path. It wouldn't look at me then, it just came out on the road and trudged along. It was just him and me, that was the feeling I got. I truly wished him well. Now when I drive along the motorway to Malmö and see one of the beautiful, black-and-white-snouted badgers lying bloodied and motionless on the roadway, I am filled with a dull, hopeless rage, for the thing that killed it is a structure that I help to maintain and which works so well for me that I am unwilling to renounce it. And even if I were to do so, if I stopped driving a car, it wouldn't change anything, neither the rising global temperature nor the dead animals in the road. It is an original sin, it belongs to everyone and can only be undone by all of us together.

Infants

Holding an infant close to one's body is one of the great joys in life, perhaps the greatest. This is when the child is newborn and so tiny that the adult's palms nearly cover its little body completely, when its gaze seems to float and only rarely fastens on something in its surroundings, and one senses that for the baby being in the world is almost exclusively sensual: the warmth and softness of the body that the infant nestles against, the lukewarm milk that fills its tummy, sleep which overcomes it so deliciously every few hours. For the newborn infant, everything revolves around equalising the differences between itself and the surroundings, getting everything warm, close, soft. A sudden drop in temperature opens a chasm between the infant and reality, so does a sudden sound or a sudden movement, and it screams.

Satisfying these simple demands is a pleasure because they are simple, because doing so involves an interaction, a rhythm, a song, and because the closeness it requires fulfils a wish which is almost a desire: to protect, to give, to care for. For me, as a man, holding a child close against my body is the only physical intimacy I know of that isn't sexual. How it is for women I don't know, but that it is different is hardly an audacious claim. Perhaps that is why a man must be a whole lot of man not to become a woman when he lives with a newborn infant in near-symbiotic intimacy.

When the child has grown and is nearly a year old, everything is different except the joy of holding it close against one's body. But this happens more rarely because what is required now is the opposite, the child must – and wants to – expose itself to the chasm separating it from the world. It crawls along the floor, has certain spots it explores: an electrical cord here, a shoe rack or a vacuum cleaner there, and it seeks eye contact with other family members during meals, laughs when others laugh, waves when others wave. Its eyes are bright and lively, sometimes even crafty, often happy. Many of the words buzzing around the baby have long since been memorised and identified, but they cannot be used yet, they are stored as in a depot. So are the movements that will come later. Holding on to a table leg and slowly getting up, standing, and soon, with surprise, excitement, fear and joy filling its chest, the first steps. But when it has been out in the world on its own for long enough, maybe only ten minutes, maybe all of thirty, the child again seeks closeness, the adult body that lifts it up and holds it close. When it leans its head against the adult's chest in a gesture of total trust, the feelings that burst forth in the adult are irresistibly good. Why? I don't think it is the child's helplessness we are defenceless against, that isn't what goes straight to the heart, but rather its innocence. For one knows how much pain the world will inflict, one knows how complicated and difficult life will become and how the child will develop a whole series of defence mechanisms, avoidance strategies and methods of self-preservation in that intricate interaction with one's social environment that a full life entails, for better or worse. None of this is present in the infant, the joy that shines in its eyes is entirely pure, and the adult body it leans its head against is still the safest place it has.

Cars

For a long time I thought I wasn't the type to drive a car, that I wasn't capable, that my strength lay in sentences and abstractions, thoughts and images, while everything involving hands and feet, pedals and levers was beyond my reach. One of my recurrent nightmares was that I was in a car out on the road without a driving licence; I would wake up with the same feeling of anxiety I got when I dreamed that I had killed someone or been unfaithful. I was thirty-nine years old when I got my licence, and that whole first year, driving, especially on motorways, felt like a transgression. I always felt anxious when I handed back the key to the rental company on Sunday afternoon, not unlike the anxiety I feel when I've been drinking the previous day. It must have been the Protestant reflex that was triggered – every freedom has a price, which in my case is anxiety. For my mother, to whom I owe my Protestant heritage, driving a car is not associated with guilt, probably because it is directly linked to her work ethic; practically every day for nearly fifty years she has driven her car to and from work, by the sweat of her brow. For my father, the Protestant ethic was presumably associated with my mother's righteousness, and that he always drove too fast, always overtook other cars, was never afraid to take risks,

I now believe was an attempt to break free of all rules, all prohibitions, all duties and all undue interference in his world. Politically he was a liberal, in favour of individual liberty and opposed to a strong state, whereas my mother, obversely, was for a strong state and cared about solidarity with the weak. Do I need to add that my mother always drives slowly and carefully? As for me, I bought my first car four years ago, a white Volkswagen Multivan, which I still drive. It is large and heavy, has a small engine and takes a long time to pick up speed. I still like it, though; it has seven seats and plenty of space, and after having dented and scratched it three times during the first year, I've also learned how to park it in tight spaces. The fear of transgression has disappeared, now I drive with a clear conscience, perhaps because driving a car is no longer associated with freedom but with habit and utility. I drive fast but not very fast, and I never take risks. What I like best of all is talking to the children while I drive, for a space is created between us as we move through the open landscape out here, it's as if the distance between what they think and what they say is abolished in the car, as if they can talk to me about anything. When at the same time vast cloud massifs are hanging motionless in the blue sky out on the horizon, or rain dashes against the windscreen forming its irregular patterns, which a moment later are swept away by the wipers, I can sometimes feel intensely happy. The feeling can get particularly strong in the forest by the sea on these autumn afternoons, in the long straight passage between the trees, leafless and stark, when approaching cars come towards us in the dusk with their shining headlights, their dark panes and gleaming bodies, below the surface of which an archaic fire smoulders.

Loneliness

It's good to be alone. It's good to shut the door behind one and not be with other people for a while. It hasn't always been like this. In childhood being alone was a defect or a failing, often painful. If you were alone it was because no one wanted to be with you or because there was no one to be with. The absence of others was unequivocally negative. Several people together was good, alone was bad, that was the rule. And yet I never asked myself how this applied to my father, who spent so much time alone. He was a supreme being, everything about him was as it should be, it never occurred to me that his solitude too could be a defect or a flaw, something painful. He had no friends, only colleagues, and he spent most evenings alone in the basement recreation room, where he listened to music or worked on his stamp collection. He shunned social intimacy, he never sat on a bus, never cut his hair at a hairdresser's, he was never one of the parents who drove to football matches with a carload of kids. At the time I didn't notice this. Not until he died and we found his diary was I able to see his life in that light. Loneliness concerned him, he had thought about it a great deal. 'I have always been able to recognise the lonely,' he wrote in his diary. 'They don't walk the same way as other people. It is as if they don't carry any joy, any spark within themselves, whether they are women or men.' In another entry he wrote, 'I am looking for a word for the opposite of loneliness. I would like to find a different word to love, which is far too overworked and inadequate. Tenderness, peace of mind and soul, togetherness?' Togetherness was a good word for it. It is the opposite of loneliness. Why he never felt it I don't know. It is one of the good feelings in life, perhaps the best. And yet I often do as he did, close the door behind me to be alone. I know why I do it, it's good to be alone, for a few hours to be exempt from all the complicated bonds, all the conflicts, great and small, all the demands and expectations, wills and desires that build up between people, and which after only a short time become so densely intertwined that the room for reflection and for action are both restricted. If everything that stirs between people made a sound, it would be like a chorus, a great murmur of voices would rise from even the faintest glimmer in the eyes. Surely he too must have felt this? Perhaps more powerfully than I do? For he started drinking, and drinking muffles this chorus and makes it possible to be with other people without hearing it. Yes, that must be it. For the sentence he ended that diary entry with, I could never have written. He wrote, 'In brief, what I have just now so clumsily tried to express is that I have always been a lonely man.' Or, the thought strikes me now with horror, maybe it was the other way round? Maybe he simply didn't hear this chorus, didn't know it existed and therefore didn't become bound by it, but remained forever standing on the outside, observing how all the others were bound by something he didn't understand?

Experience

Yesterday I read a book which had a sentence that I took note of because it seemed so very young. The first-person narrator expresses his unease that lately he has been stagnating intellectually. I remember worrying about the same thing when I was in my twenties. Well, actually it was worse, for if one stagnates at least there has been a prior progression. I considered my intellectual deficiencies, the cognitive stasis that marked me, as something fundamentally unchangeable, a trait of my character. The anxiety I felt when I simply wasn't able to grasp what I was reading, for instance Julia Kristeva's book *Revolution in Poetic Language* or anything at all by Lacan. And in a sense I was right that it was a flaw, that a certain kind of knowledge at a certain level of difficulty simply wasn't for me, that I was too stupid, for in this respect nothing has changed. This spring, in the evenings when I lie reading Safranski's book about Heidegger, I just don't get his philosophical explications, I don't understand what they mean even when I exert myself to the utmost. It's worse when I try reading Heidegger's own writings. Even when I consider that Heidegger writes about being a human being and I am a human being too, so that his thoughts and insights also pertain to me, it doesn't help: I just don't have it in me. When

I was twenty-five, that certainty pained me, and if I didn't exactly repress it, I distorted it and fooled myself that it wasn't necessarily true. Back then so much in life centred on the desire to become someone, ambition was powerful, and since it is blind, a life of ambition is restricted. Though actually I think that being in one's twenties is in itself to be restricted. At that age one's vigour is great, and one looks ahead, keeps one's eyes fixed on things to come, and of the things found in one's surroundings the most important are always those that hold the most promise. At the same time, and this is the cruelty of it, this forward-looking gaze is constantly confronted with the limitations of one's character, constantly coming up against a sense of stagnation – hence the youthful fear of stagnating intellectually. To turn forty is to realise that one's limitations will last one's whole life through, but also to know that all the time, whether one likes it or not, and whether one is aware of it or not, new layers are being added to one's character, a type of knowledge and insight that isn't directed towards the future, towards what will come to pass or one day be accomplished, but towards the here and now, in the things you do every day, in what you think about them and what you understand of them. That is experience. The vigour one had in one's twenties is gone, and the will is weaker, but life is richer. Not in a qualitative sense, only quantitatively. When I read Safranski's biography of Heidegger in the evenings, I understand nothing of his philosophy, but I understand *him*, in the sense that what makes up his life doesn't seem foreign and complicated but fathomable and meaningful. And in the mornings, when the three children all have to get up, put on some clothes, maybe shower, eat something, all of them in different moods and at different stages, with different problems and joys, getting it all to run smoothly, making it all work, demands a kind of knowledge that isn't written down anywhere, which it isn't possible to acquire by reading or studying but which all parents possess, perhaps without appreciating it, precisely because it is the opposite of ambition and isn't concentrated or restricted, nor is it oriented towards something to come, a future triumph, and therefore it is nearly invisible. This is how experience works, it settles around the self like a sediment, and the self, as the possibilities open to it increase in number, becomes more and more difficult to nail down: the wisest person knows that 'I' is nothing in itself.

Lice

One of the children is sitting in front of me with her head slightly bent over the table, just beneath the lamp that hangs from the dining-room ceiling. I am combing her hair with a special comb. The teeth are long, made of metal and set so close together that all the debris lodged in her hair gets combed out. Every time I finish dragging the comb through the strands of hair, I knock its teeth against a sheet of white paper lying on the table. Sometimes a few tiny black specks tumble onto the paper. We're not entirely sure what they are, but our guess is lice eggs. If the specks are large, we stare at them for a while to see whether they're moving. *Ouch!* she says when the comb snags in her hair and I tug it to force it through. *Sorry,* I say. *But we have to do this. I know,* she says. *But you don't have to tear my hair out, do you? I know,* I say, then knock the comb against the table and see a tiny silvery creature standing on the sheet of paper, looking a little dazed. It takes a few steps across the mercilessly white expanse. *Daddy, a louse,* she says. *So I see,* I say. *So kill it,* she says. I place the outermost tooth of the comb on the tiny creature and crush it against the sheet. When we've combed through all of her hair and found another two lice, we go into the bathroom. She takes off her sweater, I place a towel over her shoulders, squirt the delousing ointment into my palm and massage it into her hair and scalp. A quarter of an hour later she is bending over the edge of the bath with her head under the spray of water from the showerhead that I'm holding while the white foaming ointment sails slowly away on a rivulet of water towards the drain. Then the procedure is repeated with the other two children before I perform it on myself. It's a lot of fuss for a tiny insect, the head louse is only a couple of millimetres long and doesn't cause any real harm, it just sucks a little blood and lays a few eggs. It lives for about a month before it dies, dries up and drops out of the hair, while its descendants continue to cause a slight itching in the scalp. A generation ago that itch was enough to make house-wives move heaven and earth: all the bedlinen was washed at ninety degrees, all combs and hairbrushes were soaked in boiling water or put in the freezer, and all caps and scarves received the same treatment. Having head lice was shameful and not something one liked to talk about. The shame was handed down from a time when lice signalled uncleanness and poverty, and there was also something animal about it: it was dogs that had fur full of vermin, and monkeys that sat around constantly scratching themselves. The first time we had lice at our house, three years ago, we weren't ashamed, we were modern people and knew that lice are simply some-thing that spreads in schools and kindergartens, in newly washed as well as dirty hair. We read on the Internet that head lice are only transmitted through direct contact with other people's hair and that it is therefore unnecessary either to boil or freeze bedlinen. That was more of a symbolic act, we gath-ered, a kind of ritual purification. But now as we sit around the breakfast table scratching ourselves like monkeys, and the lice, which arrive in the autumn, appear to have latched on to us and return after an absence of a few weeks after the delousing treatment, I am no longer modern but filled with something age-old: shame that we are a family with lice.

Van Gogh

Van Gogh wasn't really a painter. At least not if by painter we mean someone to whom painting comes easily, someone who has shown early talent and perhaps as a child drew people and nearby places in such a way that the life path that followed, attending art school, painting and drawing lessons under the tutelage of an artist, seemed obvious, if not necessarily uncontroversial, to family and friends. Neither painting nor drawing came easily to Van Gogh, and it was never self-evident to the people around him that the boy would become an artist. Not until the age of twenty-seven did he begin painting. Before that he had worked as an art dealer, a bookseller, an assistant teacher and a lay preacher. He had bad nerves and a fire burning within him, and he could find no repose in any of the professions he tried his hand at. The paintings of the early years are poor, he has no technique, the figures are lumpy, the colours dark, and the totality of the paintings, what he was trying to achieve, is mediocre. And it isn't that he is really a visionary who still hasn't mastered the technique he needs to express his visions, it is rather that he is grappling with paints simply to be able to make *something*, which can at least be *called* a painting. He has particular difficulty painting people, the human form and its bodily expressions, a difficulty that persisted throughout his brief period as an artist. Had Van Gogh lived during the Renaissance or the Baroque, or for that matter during the Impressionist era, he wouldn't have been taken seriously. He would have been the untalented friend's still more untalented friend, the one with the burning eyes, the one who drank too much and whom nobody liked, for his character traits depended on forgiveness in order to work for him, and who forgives a bad painter?

What the paintings of the Renaissance, the Baroque or the Impressionist era do is capture something of the essence of their motifs, they render something of their objective being, the thing, the face, the tree, as for instance Leonardo's ermine in the arms of a young woman, where the encounter between the animal and the human is inexhaustible, and still, five hundred years later, productive. Or the Impressionists' use of light, which fixes space to a particular moment in time and thereby suspends the fleetingness of experience, which only thus can be depicted. This emanation from objective reality is completely absent in Van Gogh's work, even when he makes his breakthrough with the avalanche of iconic paintings of his final years. His paintings of landscapes produce none of the emotions that landscapes evoke, it's as if he isn't attached to them, as if he is departing and now casts a final look upon the world. The lightness this engenders is peculiar, it resembles nothing else. The lightness doesn't lie in his technique, as with other painters, for Van Gogh lost his battle with technique, his lightness is of a different kind. By relinquishing technique he gained something else, a carelessness that allows the world to appear unfettered by how we happen to have conceived of it. Van Gogh tried to commit himself to the world but couldn't do it, he tried to commit himself to painting but couldn't do it, therefore he rose above them both and committed himself to death; only then did the world and painting become possible for him. For the entire force of these paintings, all their manic light and singular power of penetration, which make them appear as though the celestial were suffusing the earthly and lifting it up, is contingent on the look he casts upon it really being his very last.

The Migration of Birds

One autumn afternoon I take the clean crockery out of the dishwasher while I am frying sausages and cooking macaroni, and when the dishwasher is empty, I load it with the breakfast plates. I shovel half a bowl of oatmeal squares which have soaked up so much milk that they've almost dissolved into the waste bin, and a tin of liver paste that has been scraped clean, tie the tops of the bag, lift it out of the bin, turn down the heat on the stove and go out carrying the bag in my hand. It's drizzling, the sky is grey and the air perfectly still. Somewhere above me there is a honk, then another, and I look up. Maybe ten geese are flying by in V-formation. I can hear their wingbeats as they lie on the air with their outstretched necks and undulating movements. When they have flown past, I continue over to the rubbish bin, drop the bag into it and stand for a moment looking out at the garden, yellow and brown and pale green. Everything in it shimmers with moisture. If I walk out onto the lawn, I know that my heels will sink into the grass and down into the ground.

In the kitchen the slices of sausage have developed a brownish-black crust from the heat, especially at the edges, and they've swollen a little and are bulging. The macaroni, which is swirling around on the eddies of seething water, is done. I pour it into a colander in the sink, toss it. Within me the migrating birds are living a life of their own. I'm not thinking of them, but they are there, in the stream of sensations and feelings which at times freeze into images. Not clear and distinct images, as with photographs, for that isn't how the external gets depicted within us, but as if in rifts: a few black triangles, a sky, and then that sound, of several pairs of wings beating up in the air. That sound awakens feelings. What kind of feelings? I ask myself now, as I write this. I know them so well, but only as feelings, not as thoughts or concepts. The sound of birds' wings beating maybe fifteen metres up in the air, heard twice or thrice every autumn for forty years.

Once, in childhood, the world was boundless. Africa, Australia, Asia, America, these were places beyond the horizon, far away from everything, with inexhaustible reservoirs of animals and landscapes. That one could actually travel there was as unthinkable as that one might journey into one of the many books I read at that time. But slowly – for it didn't come to me as a sudden insight – I began to understand what the migration of birds signified. That they flew all that way under their own power, and that the world wasn't boundless but limited, and that neither the place they left nor the place they arrived at were abstract but concrete and local.

Yes, that is what I sensed as I wedged the spatula under the slices of sausage and placed them on the green serving dish, then poured the macaroni into a glass bowl. The world is material. We are always in a certain place. Now I am here.

Oil Tankers

Nearly all my dreams are set in landscapes I moved away from long ago, as if I had left something behind there that was never concluded. Arendal, the little town in the far south of Norway on the outskirts of which I grew up, and which I left more than thirty years ago, is especially the setting of many dreams.

If one looks at pictures of Arendal from the end of the nineteenth century, the many masts in the harbour feature prominently. Arendal was a shipping town. It was home to shipowners and sailors, and although most of the ships carried timber from the great inland forests to the Continent and Great Britain, and mainly sailed the North Sea shipping routes, they were part of a worldwide network, the coordinates of which also included exotic and faraway lands such as China and Borneo. A slave ship sank just off the coast of Arendal in the eighteenth century; a ship in distress with Wagner on board sought refuge in its port at the beginning of the nineteenth century, an event described in *The Flying Dutchman*, and it was from Arendal that Fridtjof Nansen set sail on his very first expedition to the Arctic.

When I grew up there, in the 1970s, all of this was gone. No masts in the harbour, no big ships sailing through the

Galtesund sound other than the ferry to Denmark. True, there was a maritime college in Arendal, and shipyards, and both shipowners and captains lived there still, but maritime culture no longer dominated the town; it was on its way out, or it had become private and purely for recreation, as shown by the myriad of small boats cruising the waters beyond the town during the summer half of the year and thronging the archipelago on sunny days.

But then something happened. The oil crisis erupted, and the enormous oil tankers that nominally belonged in Arendal, being owned by local shipping companies, and which roamed the seas and had never appeared in their home town, no longer received orders. Now they came home. Suddenly one day there they were, anchored in the sound between the islands of Hisøya and Tromøya. They were gigantic. They reared up above the houses and the hillsides, and were visible from everywhere, like something from another age. Although they were made of metal and the products of technology and engineering science that hadn't existed only a few generations earlier, it wasn't the future they seemed to have come from, but the past. Perhaps because they at once seemed so simple and primitive and were so huge that, at a time when everything else was becoming smaller and smaller, they had to have come from the depths of the past, the abode of gods. They didn't belong there, but they were more beautiful than anything else and impossible to take one's eyes off for the first few weeks. They lay completely motionless, as if closed in on themselves, there were no entrances to them, nothing that opened them up, they rejected everything. More than forty years after I first saw them, they still live within me: I dreamed about them last night. I was standing near the maritime college and gazing out over the sound between the two islands where the oil tankers lay at anchor. The next moment I was close up against them. Transfixed, I saw a hull tower above me like a mountainside, and an anchor, thick as a tree trunk, vanishing mutely into the deep. Dreams belong to an ancient substratum within us and constitute a form of consciousness that we have in common with animals. When I woke up, it occurred to me that this must be how our world appears to them, that this is how animals perceive all our constructions, all our skyscrapers, bridges and vessels. For in my dream the oil tankers meant nothing, they were just there, while at the same time the impression they made filled me entirely.

Earth

Late this afternoon, when darkness had begun to fall and I was on my way home from school with the children, I saw lights creeping forward slowly out in the fields, they were tractors. Further on, at the edge of the plain where the road makes a ninety-degree turn, we passed one of them at close range. It was standing still, and the beams from its powerful headlights opened a large grotto in the darkness. The earth, black, in some places glistening, extended like a floor. I found myself thinking of the earth as being alive, that it is in hibernation during these months and comes to life again in spring, when it seems to rise towards the sky in all its various expressions: bright yellow oilseed rape fields, pale green cornfields, which as summer progresses turn yellow-beige and gradually plain beige, yellow-green pastures, sharp green plots of onions, potatoes, carrots, sugar beet. And that the earth after this huge exertion once again seeks rest, and without a murmur of protest allows everything to be cut down, pulled up and harvested, and then again lets itself be ploughed so delightfully before the restfulness of winter.

But of course that's not how it really is. The earth is dead – or non-living, which is perhaps a more accurate description of its essential state. The earth is non-living, but it contains life and in this it resembles the ocean, which is also non-living but contains life. In contrast to the water in the ocean, a purely chemical compound of two elements, hydrogen and oxygen, which other substances and minerals float around in but never penetrate, and which cannot change without becoming something else, earth is both impure and mutable. Earth is not what comes to be, but what is left over, it is composed of remains, such as sand left over from stone, organic material left over from animals and plants, and of minerals that have leached into it or have been blown there, and of gases and liquids. And while water is transparent and neutral, the colour of the earth is black, like night and all that doesn't exist. That it is precisely from the earth that life should burst forth every spring, and with such wild force as if it sought to escape the death in which it is rooted, at times makes me think that there must be some truth in the old Gnostic notion that the earth and life on earth were created by a demiurge. Who else could have come up with the idea of fashioning the first human being out of clay and calling him Adam, which is the Hebrew word for earth?

Even though we are not attached to the earth with roots, but are able to walk about on top of it, yet we are inseparably bound to it, both in that its transformative power upholds us and, as it were, moves us about with its force, and in that, when life ebbs away and the earth's force no longer sustains us, it draws us down towards itself in a gruesome final embrace, before we not only become like it, but become it.

As we passed the tractor, a man appeared from behind it and climbed into the driver's cab. In the rear-view mirror I saw the tractor drive off into the field and then, as we neared the other end of the long plain, shine its lights like a boat far out on a pitch-black sea.

Letter to an Unborn Daughter

22 October. A quite exceptionally beautiful day today. Sun, half-clouded sky, soft light pouring over the open landscape, where everything was glowing, especially the grass, which is still green and which makes such a contrast with the trees' autumnal colours, as if two different seasons were present at the same time. The sky was luminous, its colours pale, but the light it sent down over the fields was deep and full. I stopped at Björn's house on the way to school, we sat outside in our shirtsleeves, drinking coffee and smoking. From the hills by the sea, maybe four kilometres away, a deep booming echoed at regular intervals, an ominous, almost archaic sound, and the crackle of machine-gun volleys, all from the military training ground, which stretches away inland from Hammar. Green hills that end abruptly in sandy cliffs maybe fifty metres above the Baltic Sea. When I drove on to pick up the children, I saw that the red warning flag had been hoisted there. Four summers ago we rented a house at the foot of that hill, we holidayed there for ten days, and that's when we found the house we are living in now, the house you'll grow up in. Everything that happened before you were born will maybe come to seem almost mythical to you; I can imagine you asking your siblings for details, at the

same time not being quite able to conceive of a time before you existed.

When I think of my father, who is dead and whom you will therefore never get to meet, it is striking how little I know about his life before he married and started a family, and how incurious I was about it when I was growing up. The same goes for my mother, your grandmother, but her I can still ask – about what it was like growing up just after the war, for instance, or what they were actually taught at school. Whom she was in love with before she met my father, what kind of people they were. For that's how it is, it's our own time that matters to us, at least when we are children and adolescents, and it's what people are like then that is important, not what they bring with them from before, nor from where. I'll be forty-five when you are born, and that means I can't expect to share more than thirty years with you, and during the last of these I might be ill or feeble. If you ever have children, it might be that you have them when I am no longer here. In a way, there is also something beautiful about that, that you will continue far into the future, and your children even further, and your grandchildren, for whom this – the house you grew up in, the family you were a part of – will be no more than vague and hazy imaginings. But the grass will be green, the sky will be blue, and the rays of the sun rising in the east will flood the landscape and make it shine in every colour, for the world doesn't change, only our conceptions of it.

Today Linda told me you were kicking, and when I laid my hand against her belly I felt it, the pressure of your little foot.

Four months remain until the due date. A cot is standing ready, and a pram – I picked up both last weekend from some friends in Malmö. We threw or gave away all the baby equipment we had for the others; we didn't expect to need it again.

Now we're just here waiting. Your sisters and brother have seen an ultrasound image of you, and they've drawn pictures for you. They're looking forward to your arrival.

So am I.

NOVEMBER

Tin Cans

Tin cans are made of metal and are usually shaped like a
cylinder, a form not found in nature, not even on a pebble
beach, where the ocean over the course of millions of years
has ground the stones against each other into every con-
ceivable variation of spheres and cones without ever having
produced the regular shape of the can, with a flat circle at
each end connected by a tube. If one finds a tin can in nature,
one is never in doubt as to what it is, it can't be mistaken for
anything else, but lies there in the heather, lies there on the
beach, lies there in the ditch as something uniquely itself,
absolutely isolated from its surroundings. In this sense there
is a correspondence between the shape of the can and its
function, which is to shut something off from the world. Or
rather, from the course of the world, what we think of as
time, the processes that every thing which exists is subject
to. Whatever is inside the tin can is shut off from those substances and gases and organisms that are continually at work
to dissolve matter, whether they cause the matter to rust,
to rot or in other ways to change its form and consistency.
The space inside the tin can is airtight, and whatever is kept
in there is exactly as it was at the time it was sealed in. In
the cupboard, where tin cans are stored, the forces of nature

ravage everything else: hot dog rolls that are kept there get covered in a thin layer of bluish mould, start to smell and become inedible, the same goes for tortillas, while taco shells turn soft, and soft drinks that have passed their expiry date become sour and undrinkable. Peas, sweetcorn, pineapple and *lapskaus* stand aloof from all this in their time capsules. It is the same principle that caused the Swedish warship *Vasa* to be preserved as the only extant seventeenth-century ship in the world – it lay in oxygen-poor waters covered by silt and clay – and the same principle that enabled the so-called bog bodies of Denmark, human corpses from the Stone Age, to be exhumed from the bogs in such good condition that they might have been only recently interred there. Nothing can live in airtight space, therefore nothing can die in it either. When one looks at tin cans without their labels, just plain metal fashioned into this inorganic shape, they have a machine-like and industrial look, it is obvious that their purpose is to reject life. While this cold, lifeless appearance might not bother anyone in an emergency or in extreme conditions, such as at the front during a war, it isn't something anyone would opt for if they had a choice, such as in a supermarket shopping for food. That is why all tin cans are provided with labels, which not only state what they contain, for instance PEAS – for language too has an element of coldness and lifelessness that is unable to conquer the inimical metal – but in addition feature pictures of the freshest and most delectable sort, so that we pass over the metal and the dead space, and go straight from the newly harvested peas to the peas in the serving dish. In fact, when the tin opener has sawn through the metal top and I have bent it back, so that it rises like a jagged visor above the opening in the can, my mouth waters at the sight of the small, round, dark green peas lying there in their transparent, slightly viscous brine. They taste so much better and richer than pale frozen peas, the taste seems darker somehow and is perfect as an accompaniment to fish fingers, for example, together with boiled cauliflower and grated carrots, potatoes and butter.

Faces

It is difficult to imagine anything we have more knowledge about than faces. It is also difficult to imagine a knowledge that is more equally distributed. Seeing is not only registering, it is also differentiating. While everyone can see that what is growing in the meadow is a tree, and while almost everyone can see that it is an apple tree, only a select few are privileged to see what kind of an apple tree it is, how old it is, what condition it is in. Almost all areas in our lifeworld require some form of competence and experience in order to be seen and understood. Not so with faces. The moment we see a face, we know whether we've seen it before, even though it may have been only once, a long time ago. We know what it expresses, whether it is joy or sorrow, surprise or indifference, eagerness or sluggishness. We also know straight away how old it is and whether it could be considered beautiful or ugly, plain or special, and whether we like it or not. And even if we find that it resembles another face, we rarely mistake it, we perceive every single face as being unique, even the most ordinary of the ordinary. In a way this is peculiar, since all faces are made up of the same components, which are not many at all. Forehead, eyebrows, eyes with eyelashes, nose, cheeks, mouth with lips and teeth, chin. We differentiate out of necessity, we need to be able to distinguish between edible and inedible plants, for example, and also out of interest, which when it is great, comes naturally: anyone with the slightest interest in art is able to tell at first glance whether a painting is by Van Gogh or Gauguin, Morisot or Pissarro. That everyone has equal knowledge about faces is due to necessity and interest as well as closeness, and what this tells us is that our real lives are not lived in landscapes, nor among objects, but in the human realm, in the light of the human face. That the Enlightenment and its efforts to rationalise the lifeworld eventually led science to the human face, so that early in the twentieth century distances and sizes began to be measured and fitted into larger systems of classification, together with colours and other subtle differences, in the same way that plants and animals were classified, or the various expressions of the human face were catalogued by drawing them in series, is therefore not the least bit surprising. But since the face not only belongs to the human realm, unlike an arm or a finger it also expresses it, it cannot be captured. Whatever is human is changeable, it is mobile, and it is unfathomable. Just this morning I was sitting in the living room and cast a glance at my oldest daughter's face, which is by far one of the faces I know best, in all its phases, ages and expressions. Her face lay with its cheek pressed against the armrest of the sofa, eyes turned towards the television. In it I saw something new: it resembled my mother, which it had never done before. The next time I glanced at it, the resemblance was gone. As for me, these days I look almost exactly like my father.

Pain

An essential aspect of pain is that it is untranslatable. We can see that someone is in pain, and we can understand that it hurts, but the distance between the concept of pain and pain itself is so great that not even the deepest compassion can bridge it; we are for ever strangers to the pain of others. This means that the person in pain is always alone. But pain isn't merely untranslatable from one person to another, but even within a single person, for as soon as the pain ceases, the same distance arises in ourselves: we remember that it hurt, and we can tell ourselves that the pain was like a darkness that submerged us, and in this way we can fathom it by thought, but thoughts exist in a world apart where everything is weightless and immaterial, for the moment pain returns and it starts to hurt again, the thoughts are drawn aside like a curtain, and we are once again in the real: *Oh no, that's how it was.*

It is therefore easy to imagine that pain belongs to the flesh, and that it exists at a different and more straightforwardly corporeal level of reality than thought. But that isn't the case. For if the cause of pain has its origin in an event in the flesh and is therefore material, pain itself is immaterial, something that arises in the brain, where signals from nerve fibres produce an electrochemical reaction in cells which causes the pain to flare up, as it were, with a strength and an intensity that are to our regular thoughts as burning magnesium is to the light from a ceiling lamp. It *feels* as if the pain is closer to physical reality also because it is felt in the body, in the place where it hurts, whether it is in the hand, which has been crushed by a rock, or in the kidney, where the cancerous tumour is growing, and not in the brain, where thoughts are centred.

But just how far pain is a construct, and how closely it is related to thought, becomes clear when one knows that pain can also arise in limbs or body parts that no longer exist. The flesh is gone, the leg has been amputated, but pain recreates what no longer exists; the patient distinctly feels the leg, which is no longer there. The leg is a fiction, and in this way pain reveals its kinship to thought, but also its superiority, for if thought creates fictions we are ready to believe in, we never experience them as physical realities.

The relationship between pain and reality becomes even more complicated when we consider the pain we sometimes feel in dreams: what status should we assign to that? One night this spring while I was sleeping I got a terrible stomach ache. It was quite unbearable, as if a hand was ripping out my entrails. I lay writhing, nothing else existed except this pain. Then suddenly everything returned to normal. I lay in bed with my eyes open and felt endlessly relieved, the way one does when pain lets up. Had I been sleeping? Yes, I must have been. Was the pain just a dream? I didn't know for sure, but many things seemed to indicate that it was. So what kind of pain was it if it was able to leap from reality to dream with all its strength intact? What is then revealed is the very nature of dreams, which is nothing other than the emergency preparedness of the imagination, whose task it is to build a model of reality, for which it may employ every branch of consciousness, which in turn has the model at its disposal, for it is there that we live, in a representation of reality, an inner simplification.

To us there appears to be a relation of identity between the inner image and the outer reality, but once in a rare while a fissure develops, as when we feel pain in something that doesn't exist, or when we get the distinct sensation that we have experienced before what we are experiencing now – what we call déjà vu, which is nothing other than a miniscule displacement in the identity between our image of reality and reality itself.

Dawn

The houses here lie in a horseshoe with its opening towards the east, so that every morning all year round I can see the sunrise. It's a sight that is hard to get used to. Not that it is surprising, for of course I know that the sun rises every morning, and that its light makes the darkness yield, but rather because it happens in so many different ways, and perhaps most importantly that it feels so fundamentally good. The feeling is a little like taking a hot bath when one is feeling chilly, satisfaction that the body is somehow restored to its basic state. When the basic state has been re-established, the satisfaction disappears, we rarely think about the fact that our body temperature is perfectly regulated. The same is the case with the sunrise. It isn't the light in itself that feels good, for once it's here, say, at around 2.30 in the afternoon, we take it for granted. What matters is the actual transition. Not the light from the immobile sun, which shoots across the horizon as the earth's sphere turns towards it, but the faint glow cast by this light in the minutes before, visible as a pale streak in the darkness of night, so faint it almost doesn't seem to be light at all, merely a kind of enfeebling of the darkness. How this infinitely subtle, dim, grey-marbled gleam slowly spreads out and imperceptibly enters the garden around me, where the trees and the walls of the houses just as slowly emerge. If the sky is clear, it turns blue in the east, and then the first beams of sunlight shoot forth, bright orange. At first it is as if they are just showing off and don't have any other attributes than this colour, but the next moment, when the rays plummet in vast chutes across the landscape, they show their true qualities, filling the landscape with colours and brightness. If the sky isn't clear but overcast, all this happens as if by stealth: the trees and the house emerge from the darkness, which vanishes, and the landscape fills with colour and brightness but without the source of this transformation being visible as anything more than an area of greater luminosity in the sky, sometimes round, if the cloud cover is thin, sometimes indeterminate, when it seems as if the clouds themselves are shining. Through this phenomenon, which occurs every single day of our lives, we also understand ourselves. Dawn is always the beginning of something, as its opposite, dusk, is always the end of something, and when we consider that in practically every culture darkness represents death and evil, while light represents life and goodness, these two transitional zones between night and day become manifestations of the great existential drama we are caught up in, which is something I rarely think about as I stand in the garden gazing towards the growing light in the east, but which must still resonate in me somehow, since watching it feels so good. For darkness is the rule and light its exception, as death is the rule and life its exception. Light and life are anomalies, the dawn is their continual affirmation.

Telephones

So slow is the internal processing of reality that when I think of telephones, the image that comes to mind is still the grey standard model in use in Norway in the 1970s and 80s. It was made up of two parts, the first being a faintly curved tube which widened into a sort of hemisphere at either end, the latter perforated by little holes in the discs covering them. One of the hemispheres was pressed against the ear, inside it was a receiver from which issued the voice of the person one was calling, the other one was held in front of the mouth, since it contained a microphone that picked up one's own voice and transmitted it. The second part of the telephone was the actual apparatus, connected to the handset by a spiral cord. The apparatus customarily stood on a table, and was dominated by a rotary dial with a hole for each of the ten digits made to fit the index finger. At the top it had a cradle, which the handset rested on when it wasn't in use. On the cradle were two white plastic plungers, which regulated access to the outside line. When the handset rested on them, they were pushed down and the line was cut, while they slid up when the handset was lifted, thereby opening the line. A uniform unbroken tone was then heard in the earpiece of the handset. If one dialled the number of the person one wished to talk to on the finger wheel, the tone changed. Either a series of short tones sounded – that meant the line was busy – or else one heard a series of somewhat longer tones, in which case the line was open, and if the handset at the other end was then lifted, one could begin to speak.

In itself this was a perfect construction, extremely functional, adapted to its purpose in the simplest imaginable way, while it was also sophisticated, given its ability to transmit voices back and forth all over the globe. But since it has now all but disappeared, it can't have been without certain weaknesses. These were not of a technical nature, nor were they inherent in the design of the telephone, but rather in the distance which it established. Since access to telephones was regulated – in Norway at the beginning of the 1970s there was a queue to obtain a telephone line, and it might take several years from the time one applied to its actual installation – and since there was only one outside line from each house, the telephone radiated a certain authority, a certain solemnity. Moreover, telephoning was expensive, especially trunk calls, to say nothing of international calls, which were rare, for the grey standard telephone existed at a time when people neither travelled abroad much nor knew many people who lived outside the country's borders. Children might make prank calls, that is dial a random number and say some nonsense, and teenagers might talk on the phone with each other for hours, but these were transgressions, which was precisely why they occurred. If anyone called after ten o'clock at night or before nine o'clock in the morning, they were either drunk or someone had died. The telephone upheld a certain formality, it contained within it a permanent distance, and since this was owing to its shape, which even frequent use was powerless to overcome, the shape had to be changed, since the times were tending towards greater informality. The same thing happened to the letter. Old people, into whose lives the stationary telephone had sunk deep roots, treat the mobile phone just as formally and with the same respect, which gives them an air both ridiculous and touching. Distance, which was formerly a means to control reality, so as not to appear awkward or inept, has now itself become awkward, and while the two are hardly comparable, I find myself thinking of the figure of the dictator, one day all-powerful and controlling every aspect of life, the next, when the people revolt, completely naked and exposed.

Flaubert

Ever since I began to read the books in my parents' bookcase at the age of ten or eleven – what I then called adult books – Flaubert and Tolstoy have been my companions. Tolstoy because I read a two-volume biography of him that belonged to my mother, Flaubert because I read *Madame Bovary*. I can't have understood much of *Madame Bovary* and can no longer remember what it was like, but I assume that what attracted me to these books was the different worlds they opened up, tsarist Russia and the emperor's France in the middle of the nineteenth century. I must have read *Madame Bovary* in the same way I read all those other French novels, like *Twenty Years After* and *The Three Musketeers*, or for that matter *The Red and The Black*, which stood on the same shelf. The subject matter was of no importance, it was the atmosphere I was after, which in those nineteenth-century novels for me was associated with landscapes: dusty roads, horses gleaming with sweat, mills, rivers, the deep shade of leafy trees, little villages. *Madame Bovary* gave me all that, to read it as an eleven-year-old was like walking out into a cool, clear, early-summer morning, when the sea lies smooth and still, the trees stand motionless and the sky is a deep blue, seemingly endless, with the sun slowly climbing the horizon. When I read it again as a student, it was as an example of the realist novel, in which the author has withdrawn from the narrative completely and only the objective descriptions of places and events remains. We learned to be suspicious of this realism; its conception of language as a sort of window that one could see through was both false and naïve. I studied literature in the heyday of linguistic materialism and post-structuralism, when the ideal was to penetrate so deeply into the words' own reality that all notions of author, biography, intention and actual surroundings were suspended. Though my own experiences as a reader were based precisely on this, on seeing straight through language into the reality they created, I was also fascinated by the inherent weight of words; their relation to the greater picture resembled the way atoms related to the visible world: independent of everything else, they whirled about on their own, forming clusters which weren't called molecules but rather sentences, in accordance with their own laws, which sitting raptly in the university reading hall one might painstakingly tease out with a sense of belonging to the future. Since then I have read *Madame Bovary* several times. One summer my copy was left on the lawn for a couple of nights, I had been lying there reading and had forgotten it, but even when I noticed it later on, I didn't bring it inside, there was something so pleasing about the sight, the green grass growing up along the edge of the scarlet spine, the cover with the woman dressed in white lying in the flickering spots of sunlight filtering through the leaves of the apple tree. When I finally pulled myself together and picked it up, the spine was crooked, it must have become damp from the night dew and then dried out. *Madame Bovary* is the world's greatest novel, there's no doubt in my mind; it has a sharpness, a crystal-clear feeling of physical space and materiality which no novel either before or after it has even come close to matching. Flaubert's sentences are like a rag rubbed across a windowpane encrusted with smoke and dirt which you have long since grown accustomed to seeing the world through. The feeling you get then, when for the first time in a long while the world shines brightly again.

Vomit

Vomit is usually yellowish and can range from pale yellow to yellowish-brown, with certain areas of quite different colours, like red or green. Its consistency is fluid and varies from relatively firm and porridge-like to completely runny, like soup. The initial burst of vomit is usually coarsest in texture, a moist mass containing small pieces and lumps, while the final vomit, given that it comes in a series, can consist merely of a yellow liquid, sticky and gelatinous like raw egg white. Contrasted with the white, smooth porcelain of the toilet bowl and its clear water, it should be possible to consider vomit, at times a fiery yellow, nearly ablaze, at other times paler, the colour of straw, something beautiful, not least when its liquid elements, dissolved in gastric juices, mix with the water in slowly swirling clouds or spirals of yellow. Vomit on parquet flooring, with the contrast between the hard shiny surface of the wood and the soft moistness of the vomit spreading over it, not unlike a landslide at the bottom of a valley, might conceivably be thought of as beautiful too. Not least because the rule governing beauty holds that it is a category usually reserved for the rare and exceptional. But where vomit is concerned, there are two factors which trump the rule about exceptionality, and these are that vomit is unfinished, a concretisation of the pejorative term *undigested*, and that it belongs with the liquids and substances of the body, the shit, the piss, the spit, the sperm and the snot, which all have in common that to a greater or lesser extent they are considered offensive, and when they derive from other people's bodies, repulsive. Regardless of the beautiful gradations of yellow that piss, or of green that snot, possesses, neither piss nor snot stand a chance against the fact that they come from the interior of the body and are associated with waste matter. Personally, I have wiped up all kinds of vomit, from the dog's to the cat's and from the children's to my own, and I have always found it disgusting – the smell, the colour and the texture. Especially revolting is the vomit that comes right after a meal, where for example chunks of pizza are still intact and recognisable, and then it has struck me that this reaction is odd, since pizza, or pizza topping, itself looks like vomit. Eating vomit is unthinkable, it would be physically impossible, the gagging reflex would cause it to be re-vomited, probably the very moment the soft porridge filled the mouth. This reaction is so powerful it can't be based on cultural conditioning, it must belong to the body and its physiology, the instinct that protects us against eating something tainted and poisonous. My children have all been afraid of that impulse, whenever they have felt sick, they have started to cry or even to wail piteously. When they were very young it wasn't like that, then vomiting was just something that happened, like the time I was on my way home from the kindergarten with one of them, it was in the afternoon, the sky was dark and the bus was full of silent people returning from work. She sat next to me, and suddenly, without any warning, she threw up on me. It was a cascade, vomit covered all of one side of my jacket. She looked up at me in alarm when it was over. A kindly fellow passenger fumbled in her handbag for some paper tissues and handed me a few, but they weren't much help, they were so small and puny against the overwhelming quantity of puke. I pulled the cord, and we got off at the next stop. The stench filled my nostrils, and vomit was dripping slowly off my jacket, but it was neither disgusting nor uncomfortable, on the contrary I found it refreshing. The reason was simple: I loved her, and the force of that love allows nothing to stand in its way, neither the ugly, nor the unpleasant, nor the disgusting, nor the horrific.

Flies

The flies have disappeared. It must have happened several weeks ago, but I only noticed it today, when I cleaned the table with a cloth before breakfast, and while I was at it did the windowsills, where there lay a dead fly, light and dry as a tiny fallen flower petal. I swept it up in the cloth, and a few seconds later it fell without a sound down into the sink and was swirled around by the streaming water together with the rest of the dirt when I turned the tap on, before it glided through one of the small holes at the bottom and vanished.

In the summer the house is full of them, especially the kitchen, where they sit everywhere rubbing their feet together or buzz restlessly back and forth. I usually leave them in peace until there are so many of them that I suddenly lose all composure and start killing them with the fly swatter. One swipe and the fly instantly lose its grip and tumbles from the white roof beam – like one shipwrecked who, clinging to the gunwale of a lifeboat, suddenly gives up and lets go, I sometimes think then as the other flies take off agitatedly and fly somewhere else. Whether they understand what is going on I have no idea, but they behave as if they do, for after I have finished off the first five or six, they suddenly become hard to find, as they seem to seek out dark surfaces, against which they are almost invisible.

Flies are in many respects extremely advanced beings. Some can fly at a speed approaching a hundred kilometres per hour, others can cover distances of more than ninety kilometres without pause. But what truly distinguishes them is their myriad of eyes, there can be thousands of them, and in some fly species they cover almost their entire head. These eyes, called ommatidia, are hexagonal and set very close together in constructions that appear more mechanical than organic, like something that might have been assembled in an electronics factory. What the flies are able to see through them is hard to tell: whether inside the flies' heads reality is sharply and clearly outlined, or only movements, blurred and shadowy, like film replayed in fast motion. Either way, their compound eyes enable flies to perceive danger with such a margin that they have time to fly off before it reaches them. Another remarkable trait of flies is their sense of taste, since their taste cells are distributed over their entire body, and not, as with us, concentrated in the mouth. Therefore, they need only to stick their foot into what they want to eat to find out how it tastes. Taken together, these two faculties must fragment their world immensely, for if the reflection of a room is picked up by their whole head, then their attention must be directed outwards to such a degree that to flies there can hardly be any difference between themselves and the room they are in, and when everything they brush against is also tasted, it must seem still less clear to them what is them and what is the world. Still, they must have some sort of self-awareness, if only in the form of the instinct that makes them fly off when danger approaches.

This compact, acutely sensate and swift-moving creature lives only about half a year, a single summer season, and in many respects a lifespan that brief appears meaningless, considering the sophistication of its bodily and sensory structures. But on reflection it isn't, for the lack of a separate identity and the fact that their self-awareness is so feeble that it almost merges with the room they are in both make any accumulation of experience impossible, so that flies are perfectly interchangeable, and if one wishes to understand their nature, no doubt the principal thing is that to flies it doesn't matter who is a fly as long as they're flies. That's why they come pouring out of their warm shelters at the beginning of summer in an endless stream stretching back millions of years, into our kitchens and living rooms. And maybe this is what Leonardo da Vinci was thinking of when he wrote in his notebooks that flies are the souls of the dead. The dead have lost their selves, and without their selves they are nothing but space, at one with the world they will continue for all eternity to be born into and to die away from, like flies.

Forgiveness

Progress is impossible to measure, since the value of change is so relative and depends entirely on the place from which it is viewed and understood. As regards the material world, change itself is incontestable, for example that some people at a certain point in time turned from hunting and gathering whatever food they could find to cultivating the soil and raising livestock in a new, sedentary form of existence. Or that some people at a certain point began to produce clothes by means of machinery, which radically altered the structure of their economy, since the production of goods was no longer limited by the capacity of the individual or the single household. Previously each had produced whatever they themselves used, and any surplus was sold or traded locally, but now they were liberated from spatial constraints, unlocking the limitless potential that lay in the monetary system.

These changes are factual, but their evaluation is not. As regards progress in the immaterial world – that which has to do with interpersonal relations – not only is the value of change relative, but even change itself. This is so because everything that concerns the spirit and the soul is only revealed indirectly and must consequently be interpreted, and because the people affected by the changes, if they happened long ago, were confined within another language with different patterns of thought to ours, making it by no means obvious that even an identical sentence, spoken for instance in Norway in the year 976 and repeated in the same place in 1976, would have the same signification. We may believe that they were like us, but we can't know. We can dig up their ships and determine how they sailed them. We can unearth the foundations of their houses and determine how they lived. We can analyse their DNA and determine where they came from. But we can never determine where they stood with regard to forgiveness, or what they thought about it.

Seen from a distance of more than a thousand years, it seems as if the old lineage-based society was guided by very different parameters, in a cultural system where forgiveness simply didn't exist or was an anomaly. If one was wronged by a family member, or if someone in the family behaved basely or objectionably, one didn't take revenge, but neither did one forgive, if by forgiveness is meant a deliberate act, a thrust of mercy. It was more a case of accepting it, based on a conception of character as an unchanging entity – she is like this, he is like that. If one was wronged by someone outside the family, verbally or physically, deliberations followed concerning whether the wrong should be avenged, but the deliberations never considered whether the wrongdoer should be forgiven or not, they were exclusively concerned with what the consequences of taking vengeance would be. Maybe it would be wise to let it go, for everyone knew the destructive forces inherent in revenge and blood vengeance, but only if one could do so without loss of face. Losing face was the worst that could happen, it was worse than death, which in some cases was the only thing that could restore honour.

In such a culture the notion of forgiveness must have been a revolution, a fundamental overturning of all values. You have wronged me, but I renounce my revenge and forgive you. Many people consider this to have been an advance. That Christ's message of turning the other cheek was a revolution in human society. But the fact of the matter is that the struggle remains the same, and the outcome will be the same, only the instruments of power have changed. For the weak cannot forgive the strong, that would be meaningless. Only the strong can forgive. To forgive someone is to debase them, it is to make them lose face. If one forgives someone, and this does not cause them to lose face, then one is still a victim and the weaker party. But the secret of forgiveness is that it creates a place deep within the individual where no one else holds power, and once one reaches this place, where other people don't matter, one finds a strength that no one can take away, and it is that strength which enables one to bring the other to his knees through forgiveness.

Buttons

Buttons, those little discs that we use to fasten pieces of cloth around the body, belong to a technology so old that we rarely think of them in that context. Buttons exist outside the zone of inventions, innovations and advances, and although over the years new methods of fastening pieces of cloth have appeared, such as the zip and Velcro, buttons still hold their ground. This is so because the relation between form and function is perfect, leaving no room for improvement. A button today is more or less identical to a button in the fifteenth century. One is even tempted to say that as long as there are people, there will be buttons – but of course we can't know that, for if the button is perfected and cannot be improved upon, nevertheless it can still fall into oblivion some time in the distant future, when civilisation as we know it has collapsed. And yet even that is difficult to imagine, for the uncivilised people of the future will need clothes too, and since like ours their bodies will be roughly cylindrical, they will have to find a way to fasten their pieces of cloth around them, and if at first they tie them together, or attach, for example, a stick or a bone to one side and insert it into a loop on the other, it will probably be only a matter of time before they realise the advantages of the disc shape, or until their culture becomes so civilised that they begin to value restraint and control – for that is an important aspect of the nature of buttons – and develop garments with one or several small oblong holes on one side and corresponding little discs on the other – of bone, bronze, iron, bakelite or plastic, according to the materials their society is drawn to.

When I was growing up my mother had a large box filled with buttons. To me as a child, it was like a little treasure chest. Their round shape made the buttons resemble coins, and the many colours that shone in the light from the ceiling lamp led one's thoughts to precious stones. Sapphires, rubies, topazes, emeralds. The rustling sound they made when one poked one's fingers in among them. The feeling of opulence they gave off was ironic, since in popular parlance buttons were usually used as an example of the opposite, in expressions like *not worth a button*, and since the box of buttons was really an expression of frugality, given that it was used to replace lost buttons so as to keep garments in circulation a while longer. Buttons come in an almost infinite variety of shapes and colours, and I remember how my mother would sift through the box to find some that resembled the ones that had fallen off. So must her mother have done in her day, and her mother's mother and her mother's mother's mother. Those movements, the fingers rummaging through the mass of shiny buttons and then holding one of them close to the fabric and pricking the needle through one of the three or four little holes, with the thread dangling like a long thin tail towards the floor, they were part of a heritage, part of what linked my mother to the past, to life in the Norwegian countryside in the centuries before our time.

My children are growing up without a button box, and they have never seen their parents sew, for when a button comes loose at our house we simply discard the garment and buy a new one. I don't like this, every time it happens I am filled with a faint shadow of sorrow, that's not how things should be. But why not? Do I value frugality and poverty above abundance? Yes, in some way or other I suppose I do. Abundance is wicked, frugality is good – that too is part of the heritage. And surely few notions are more representative of civilisation than that? For if there is one thing that character-ises nature, it is abundance, a wild opulence of leaves and grass, petals and stems and branches, an unrestrained waste of chlorophyll, which the button, as it neatly and modestly yet firmly holds the shirt together, is the direct opposite of. This becomes evident on those occasions when one is overcome with desire, and with one's throat thick and one's sex throb-bing is unable to wait the time it takes to undo all the buttons, but instead grabs hold of either side of the shirt or blouse and rips it open in one violent motion, thus entering the world of the boundless, wild and wasteful. This always constitutes the greatest temptation in the realm of the buttoned-up, precisely because it is constrained and regulated by the principle of buttons. This principle does not derive from any idea, but from the hands' daily toil with the little discs, as they slowly push them edgeways into the little slits in the fabric on the other side of the shirt, straightening them once they are through so that they form a kind of lock, and thus are the technique we use both to conceal the body beneath clothing and to train ourselves in self-restraint.

Thermos Flasks

The steel Thermos looks like it was designed to be fired like a projectile and is not dissimilar in shape to an artillery shell or a shell casing. It is very beautiful. I don't find artillery shells or casings beautiful, perhaps because they are generally seen in large numbers and because there is something machine-like and one-dimensional about them. Steel Thermos flasks, on the other hand, almost always appear singly and in surroundings with which they form a strong contrast, at the bottom of a soft leather satchel, in the side pocket of a backpack, on a table in a builder's shack. The construction is simple, a hollow steel cylinder with an interior wall made of heat-insulating material, a screw top and a cap on top of that. Despite the fact that it is hard, shiny and resembles a projectile, the steel Thermos blends naturally and nearly invisibly into every setting. There is a humble air about it, probably due to the function it serves, namely to be a receptacle for hot drinks, coffee in particular, which is our most democratic and classless drink, and which is not only enjoyed by practically everyone but also at practically any time of day or night. Nevertheless, there are situations in which a Thermos will not pass unnoticed. One can take a Thermos to the workplace cafeteria without anyone batting an eye, but if one takes a Thermos on a visit to the neighbours, it will attract the attention of the entire room. This is because the Thermos represents a kind of extension of one's own home into the outside world. It doesn't present any threat in open collective spaces, either out in the woods and fields, on public transport or at places of work, but it does in other homes, whose sovereignty and rights to self-determination are challenged by the presence of the alien flask. *You're not going to bring your own coffee into our living room, are you?* This gives the Thermos a unique position among domestic items, shared only with the cool bag, another contrivance intended to maintain a constant temperature when we are on an outing or travelling beyond the confines of the home. While spatulas, saucepans, water mugs and ladles, plastic mixing bowls, whisks and hotplates stay in the kitchen and appear vaguely inappropriate in other surroundings, where they are obviously out of place – imagine a frying pan in the bathroom or an electric mixer on the lawn – the Thermos and the cool bag only come into their own outside the kitchen, where they are merely stored. Owing to its size and limited usefulness, the cool bag is more of an anomaly in everyday life, it signals something out of the ordinary and doesn't blend unobtrusively into any setting. The Thermos, on the other hand, is slender and neat, it fits in the hand, and it doesn't require any extra equipment, since the cap is also a cup; and it weaves around itself a web of associations and memories, for it was always there on car journeys, boat trips, hikes in the mountains and in the forest, connecting everything that was out there with everything back home without us ever thinking about it. Only later, when we look at all the photos from that time, does it become obvious that the Thermos is at the centre of all of them, like a kind of family totem. It discreetly embodies all that bound us together back then and which has now been broken.

The Willow

There's a willow tree outside the window. The bottom part is an old stump a little less than a metre high and divided in two by a cleft that runs down to the ground. Everything about this stump seems dead, the wood inside the cleft is soft and black, full of holes, and the top is jagged the way a tree that houses termites can sometimes appear. The bark around it is dry and cracked, like a casing with no real connection to the thing it covers. But at the top the stump divides into three short thick arms, and each of these ends in a sort of knob, from which a myriad of thinner branches shoot forth covered with smooth new bark. It is November now, and the willow will stay like this all through the winter, exactly as it was when it was pruned back earlier this autumn. Without leaves and with short branches, all gnarled and covered in knots, it looks like the interior of something which someone has brought out in order to repair and then left standing in the rain and wind. A machine of some sort – one can imagine tubes and cables connected to all the little protuberances – or the framework of some construction. Trees in wintertime are often compared to lungs, since lungs obey the same principle of form as the leafless branching limbs of trees, where each stem extends into a new one, getting thinner and thinner until the outermost fine mesh of twigs is reached. The willow doesn't look anything like a lung; instead the three knobs bear a certain resemblance to a heart, as represented in models, with the main arteries cut off and protruding like stumps from the fist-sized muscle. But the willow doesn't belong to any interior region, it doesn't sustain anything but itself, holds nothing else up. As it stands there unchanging and skeletal in winter, and then is suddenly filled with life, when the branches begin to grow and are covered in leaves, which happens faster than on any other tree I've seen, it is easy to imagine that life is merely something that is channelled through it, that it is just a kind of conduit that life is passing through, only to manifest itself triumphantly in the feast of green leaves that is the willow in summer, when the branches grow in arcs down to the ground and the dense foliage covers the trunk like a gown.

In early Christianity the dead tree growing a new shoot was a key symbol, it stood for the Resurrection, but the symbol is more ancient than that, and originally represented the continuity of life. Not only is this a humbler image, since unlike the Christian symbol individual existence is completely absent from it, but it is also truer. The willow tree is life's torchbearer, and so are we; when life is extinguished in us, it is carried on in our children.

I have no idea how old this willow tree is, but my guess is that it's roughly the same age as my mother, maybe a decade or two older. The cleft running through it wasn't there when we moved here, but one day we had a rowdy boy visiting, he climbed the willow, hung from a branch, and the trunk split. I tied a rope around it, thinking that the two halves might miraculously grow back together again, but that didn't happen. Next spring the sap shot up through two channels instead of one, and the cascade of leaves now appeared in two places, a little like when a party splits up late at night as some people drift into the kitchen, one might imagine.

Toilet Bowls

There is something elegant and graceful about the shape of the toilet bowl, even though it is heavy and massive and stands rock steady on the bathroom floor. The gracefulness comes from the fact that the toilet bowl is narrow at its base and gradually widens towards the top, so that it appears if not actually to defy gravity, then at least to run counter to it. But as is the case with many of our most beautiful objects, the toilet bowl is not made to please the eye; its form corresponds in every respect to its function, which has nothing to do with aesthetics: we piss and shit in the toilet bowl, and sometimes we even vomit. Everything about the toilet bowl is consistent with this function. That it is wide at the top and narrow at the base is because its purpose, first and foremost, is to conduct our waste matter away from the body and out of the house as effectively as possible, and as everyone who has poured liquids into bottles or cans or tanks knows, the funnel shape is unmatched when it comes to preventing slopping and spillage. And just as the funnel is never the liquids' final destination, neither is the toilet bowl; it is simply a conduit, a place of transition, a sort of transit hall for excrements. That it is made of solid porcelain, which is characterised by its smooth and hard surface, and that the interior of this surface is irrigated with water, is so that nothing should stick to it. In the toilet bowl nothing must remain, nothing must spread, everything must always be moving on. Above the bowl the cistern rises imposingly, a water reservoir, also of porcelain, often rectangular with faintly rounded edges. On top there is a button which operates a release mechanism; if it is pushed in, a little sluice gate is opened, and the water in the cistern gushes down the inside of the bowl. Instead of a button, older models sometimes have a lever on the side, not unlike a gear lever in shape, with a bakelite ball on the end, and in even older models the cistern may be separate and mounted below the ceiling, and the water in it is released by means of a handle connected to a little chain that one pulls on. At the bottom of the funnel, inside the base of the bowl, there is standing water, faintly green against the white of the porcelain, and after the piss and shit have been received into it, followed by the toilet paper, which rapidly absorbs moisture and sinks below the surface of the water, slowly capsizing, one pushes the button, and the water that gushes down the inside of the bowl flushes out everything that is lying at the bottom, and forces it through the pipes that lead out of the house, to the sewer lines beneath the street outside. That is how the toilet bowl functions, this swan of the bath chamber.

Ambulances

In the darkness on the plain the blue light of the ambulance can be seen from several kilometres away. It is unlike all the other lights in the area, both the yellow lights of the houses and the red ones blinking from the tops of windmills and telephone masts. The light of the ambulance looks like electric discharges, and it moves rapidly. It appears in the distance, vanishes for a few seconds, and when it reappears it is already a lot closer. When the darkness is dense, I sometimes imagine that it is like being inside a brain, that the unmoving lights of the farms come from clusters of cells that regulate basic functions like respiration and metabolism, while the blue light that comes racing along is a sudden idea, a terrible thought or a dream. The electric discharge is transmitted from cell to cell, it keeps coming closer, and I pull over to the side of the darkened road, for the ambulance is now only a few hundred metres away. It is driving fast, with its siren off, and this somehow increases the eeriness, for the intensity of its light seems to be magnified by the silence. Without a sound it rushes past in the darkness, and then it is gone. During the day everything is different, not just because daylight dims the blue light, but because the surroundings, the wide fields with their clusters of trees and farmhouses, the gentle incline towards the cliffs by the sea and the sea beyond somehow combine with the ambulance, metallic white against the green and grey, providing an explanation for its presence: someone has been injured or has fallen ill, now they are being taken to hospital. But even in the daytime there can be something ominous about the ambulance, which has nothing to do with what is going on inside it but with the effect it has. How car after car pulls over to the side and stops when it appears behind them. It is like the parting of a body of water, and when the ambulance speeds through the open passage, now with sirens blaring in addition to the flashing blue light, it is as if time itself has stopped for a moment, that everything outside this one movement is frozen and doesn't really exist, until the moment is past, the cars slowly start up again, and within a few seconds everything is back to normal, as if nothing had happened. Inside the ambulance time moves differently. The person lying there strapped to the stretcher doesn't notice the speed, doesn't notice the cars outside, but is inside his or her own time, which lasts a lifetime and is now about to close. The feverish activity surrounding this person, a jumble of tubes, wires, instruments, masks and syringes, also passes unperceived. In one's own separate time there are neither minutes nor seconds, neither months nor years. In our own time we are like trees, dark and motionless, at a frequency of time so low that no movements are registered other than the very greatest, such as the alternation of seasons, and even they only faintly. Thus the dying speed along the roads in the ambulance, as slowly as trees grow.

August Sander

I have been leafing through August Sander's chief work, *People of the Twentieth Century*, all morning. It is composed of several hundred portraits. They have no names assigned to them, only professions, and the photographs are grouped by social class: the peasantry, workers, the bourgeoisie. They are endlessly fascinating, both singly and taken together. I can't stop looking at them, the faces of these people who lived in Europe around the time of the First World War. Many of the faces have impenetrable expressions, somehow mute, yet they say so much, and how can that be?

The photograph not only separates an object from time, but also detaches it from space, isolating it from the relationships it is part of. The tensions felt in these photographs are due to the fact that every face, every person in them carries a charge, but what has created the charge is invisible. This explanatory deficit gives them a peculiarly enigmatic quality, it opens the closed faces, but we don't know towards what.

Many of the peasant faces are coarse, and the older they are, the coarser they look; this must be because they have spent their lives outdoors, beneath the sun, in the wind, the rain and the cold. Many have a dogged air about them, as if they are used to rejecting what comes their way, or enduring it. Many of the faces of even very young men and women, otherwise smooth and untouched by the hand of life, have this look about them. The contrast with the faces of those who lead other kinds of lives, such as the industrial magnate or the painter-artist, is striking. These faces are not coarse but refined, and not dogged but open. The thought comes easily that they must also be different on the inside. That human nature is the same in all people, but that the lives we lead cause it to flow through us in different ways. That emotions, thoughts and notions open up and are compressed in different places, depending on where and how they encounter resistance.

Some of these people must have been treacherous, some loyal, some honest, some deceitful, some God-fearing, some hedonistic. It is impossible to tell from the photographs. Everything that flowed between them is gone. Yet one gets a clear sense of who they are. So what is it that we see when we look at them?

If a photographer had come here, gathered the family on the lawn outside the house and taken our photograph, and the picture had ended up in a book which a man had opened a hundred years from now, how much of our life, as it unfolds here, would he have been able to sense?

We would have stared out at him mutely. Vanja, Heidi, John, Linda, Karl Ove. Everything that exists between us, which is all that really matters to us, would have been invisible. What he would have seen is what we ourselves don't see, that we are faces among other faces, bodies among other bodies, people among other people. And that our lives are written in our faces and in our bodies, but in a language so foreign we don't even know it is a language.

From the window where I sit writing, I look over towards the house we live in. It has two chimneys: one juts from the roof above the kitchen, the other from above the furthermost room, which we now use as an office and where I would write a few years ago. The chimneys resemble teeth, both in the way they poke out of the roof, being made of a different, harder material, and in that only their upper parts are visible. The chimneys extend down through the ceiling, and in the rooms they widen out so that at the bottom, in the kitchen and in the office, they form a whole wall of brick. But it isn't nerves that run through their hollow spaces, it is smoke, and unlike the tooth the chimney is open all the way, and on days like this, when the ground is covered with frost when we get up and the windowpanes have roses of frost along their edges, the smoke seeps slowly out of the chimney and up into the air above the house, sometimes nearly invisible, merely a quiver in the blue, sometimes thick and white like a snowdrift, in bulging patterns, sometimes grey and thin and somehow flat, like a piece of infinitely delicate cloth.

The chimney then is one of the openings of the house. But while the door is an opening for the residents, be they adults, children, cats or dogs, and for all the things the residents bring into and take out of the house, and while the windows are opened to let in fresh air, the chimney's opening is part of a closed system, the object of which is precisely to prevent that which circulates within it from penetrating the house, to keep it out. At one end of this system stands the stove, which is a small fireproof space which one gains access to through a little door. That's where one lays the wood, which one lights, and when it catches, one closes the little door, so that the smoke from the fire is led up through the chimney wall, which is built of bricks as one continuous structure and which in contrast to the rest of the house is not divided into two or three by the floors between the storeys, and eventually flows out of the upper part, which juts out of the roof and is what we think about when we think of the word *chimney*.

The chimney can never be seen in its entire length, except when a house has been burned to the ground, in which case the chimney is often the only thing left standing. The chimney dominates and controls the fire, and although the fire does its utmost to burn down even the chimney when its formidable powers are let loose, furious at having been cowed by the chimney all these years, like a foster child, one might imagine, who after having demolished everything in the room lunges at its foster father, this ordinary, boring man who never talks about anything but the importance of self-restraint and impulse control. But the fire fails to overpower the chimney, it is unable to inflict even the slightest harm on the chimney wall, and dies down at its foot. Then, as if triumphant, the chimney wall rears up into the sky from the black smouldering ruins of the house: at last everyone can see what it is capable of.

Bird of Prey

This autumn I get up early, around four in the morning, when it is completely dark and silent outside. From the window I see the garden, and the house on the other side. It is November, and it has been overcast for weeks, so no stars are visible in the sky. The light from the two lamps on the whitewashed brick wall lies in a semicircle on the flagstone path and the desolate flower beds beneath, which gleam clearly yet at the same time indistinctly in the darkness. I listen to Brahms's *Ein deutsches Requiem* and stare at the empty screen of my PC for over two hours while I smoke and drink coffee. Outside day is beginning to dawn. It doesn't feel like the light is arriving, rather that darkness is retreating. The sky above the roof of the house grows pale, it is no longer black but grey-black, while the trees lining the road up by the churchyard, maybe a hundred metres away, retain their blackness, so that as the sky lightens, they seem gradually to step forward. They no longer have leaves, only branches, thick near the trunk, thinner and thinner towards the edges of what in spring and summer is the crown of the tree, but which is now gone and exists only as a hope or a memory. And then it is day. The grass is green, the wooden wall is red, the willow's branches ochre, the stool behind it clear blue. I still haven't written anything, the screen in front of me is just as empty, and it's Saturday, so soon I will have to go and join the others. Then something happens outside the window. A bird of prey comes swooping down, it is an explosion of movement which seems to erase everything else. It lands right next to the willow, only a few metres away from me. It jabs its beak sharply into the grass with unprecedented violence, barely beating its enormous wings as if to keep its balance. My heart pounds in my chest as I watch it. Its eyes staring straight ahead as if unconnected to the head's movements, the powerful legs and the feathers growing on them, the yellow talons, the yellow beak. Large, hooked, sharp. Then it turns and seems to hurl itself into the air, beats its wings once or twice, and is already above the roof. I remain seated. This whirlwind of happenings, which while it was ongoing erased everything else, impossible to look away from, reminded me of something. But of what? Then I remember. It was during my first visit to the National Gallery in Oslo. I must have been seventeen years old. I walked around the rooms, looked at the paintings, liked them, almost all of them, especially the national romantic ones, they were magnificent, photorealistically beautiful, and the colours were marvellous. Then I entered the room where Munch's paintings hung. At a stroke, everything else paled. This was what it was all about. Art was the exception. The exception opened up the moment, broke through time and created a presence, in the vortex of which everything became meaningful. The exception is a shining light, it casts no shadow. The birds outside, those that are always here, magpies, thrushes, sparrows, now appear with a new sharpness.

Silence

One of the properties of language is that it can name what isn't here. In this way, what is out of sight can be kept within our lifeworld, and also everything that is beyond our time horizon, both what happened yesterday and what will be tomorrow. Even though the little ridge that lies just beyond my range of vision where I am sitting obviously always exists, its existence, which I have just conjured up, is related not only to the hypothetical, but also to the imaginary. You who are reading this can't know whether the little ridge really exists, even though you are seeing it now in your mind's eye, nor can you know whether I, who am writing this, exist – perhaps you are reading these words many years after they were written, and I am dead now. This tremendous expansion of the lifeworld that occurs through language, and which is maintained by it, is perhaps the principal characteristic of the human realm. Without language the world would become overgrown: every single word is like a little clearing. But it is also treacherous, in the sense that what doesn't exist – I am thinking now not of the made-up, the hypothetical or the imaginary, but of that which is the opposite of being, non-being – is given such an impossible status in language, since it transforms that which isn't anything into something simply by naming it. Nothing is what doesn't exist and which isn't anything, but if we write it or say it, it exists and becomes something: nothing. Silence is one such word, it signifies the absence of sound and is nothing in itself. But we seldom follow the word to its logical conclusion, instead we use it to qualify sound, and associate it with peace and restfulness – *It's so quiet and peaceful here*, we say when we arrive at a house in the country and the roar of traffic is gone, or when we sit down in the woods and every sound of human beings' ceaseless enterprise has died away. All we hear then is birdsong and the trees moving in the wind, which we call the silence of the forest. If it is a windless day in winter, not even that much can be heard. That silence does something to the landscape and, through it, to us. All sounds are linked to the moment, they belong to the present, that which changes, while silence is connected with changelessness, in which time does not exist. It is eternity but also nothingness, which are two sides of the same coin. I momentarily grasped what that means once when I was watching *Shoah*, a film about the extermination of the Jews, and a railway employee recalled how one afternoon the station filled with railway wagons. On board were deported Jews, children, adults and elderly people, and that evening the whole area rang with the sound of them. What kind of sounds he didn't say, but I assume it must have been children crying, male and female voices, steps, shouts, the clatter of plates, maybe even laughter. When he rode his bicycle to work the next morning all the wagons were still standing there, but now everything was silent. Not a sound could be heard. Not until I learned about that silence did I understand what the Holocaust meant, in an insight that lasted a few seconds before it vanished again. So much of life and living has to do with sound, from the patter of children's feet running across the floor, their crying and their shrieks of joy, to their regular breathing at night. But the literature about life and living is more closely related to nothing and lifelessness, night and silence, than we imagine it to be. Letters are nothing but dead signs, and books are their coffins. Not a sound has issued from this text while you have been reading it.

Drums

There is a drum kit behind me in the room where I sit writing. There is something childish about it, from the names of the individual drums, which a child might have given them – the biggest drum, which is struck with a beater attached to a pedal, is called a kick drum, the standing cymbal is called a hi-hat, and then there are two tom-toms and a floor tom-tom – to the sparkling chrome and the expectation it arouses when it is set up, of beating, banging, thumping. Visually, the drum kit is akin to the American car as it looked in the 50s, 60s and 70s, with its tail fins, brightly coloured surfaces and shiny grilles, and to the articulated lorry – not the grey, anonymous drudge with tarpaulins and company name down the sides, but the elaborate, spray-painted kind with extras, wondrous vehicles – and perhaps also the racing boat, with its gleaming hull and huge outboard engines. Everyone who saw Queen drummer Roger Taylor's drum kit when they were growing up, with its myriad tom-toms, its swarm of cymbals and the enormous enticing gong at the back, will understand what I mean. What the drum kit has in common with the American car, the bachelor's trailer truck and the speedboat, besides a look which holds a powerful attraction for children, is a promise of speed, and through it, of freedom. But what all children who begin playing the drums soon realise is that this promise is never met, for if there is anything that characterises the playing of drums, it is that it is static. Playing drums is the art of limitation, it is to renounce all excess and to purposefully pursue the path of frugality and sobriety. Of all the instruments, drums are the most ascetic. A drum kit with many drums only provides the opportunity for more of the same.

This is being written by a white middle-aged man with a frozen inner self, who walks stiffly and slightly stooped, and who never plays, never dances, never ventures into the wild, uninhibited darkness which we, following the Greeks, call Orphic, the entrance to which is through the repetition of ritual, or in other words the rhythmic. The rhythm, the beat, the thump, the trance. The heart, the blood, the sacrifice.

Drums contain both possibilities, both the Apollonian and the Orphic. So does all art, all art forms, all musical instruments, but none in a way as simple and fundamental as the drums. The Apollonian aspect lies in this, that the beats subdivide time and systematise it, in shorter and longer intervals, it is pure mathematics, as all music is always mathematics. The drumbeats must keep time precisely, like a clock, and if one launches into a transition, to indicate a break or a change of rhythm, one must be sure always to come back at just the right time. Jazz percussionists, who have turned drumming into an art, stood this relationship on its head, so that the transitions, the rupture, for them have become the actual playing, and the marking of time is merely something they drop into once in a while, by way of suggestion, like a worker who has risen in the ranks of the company and now, as its director, no longer needs to clock in but does so anyway for old times' sake. Jazz percussionists are virtuosos, there isn't a thing they can't do on the drums, they are a whole orchestra on their own, but what they create, their transgression, is more closely related to playing and games, the non-committal juggling with all existing possibilities, in other words, the Apollonian, than to that which is at the core of music, its dark heart, as simple and primitive as the straight line that hypnotises the chicken: not the beat that subdivides time, but the beat that suspends it. Time is distance, and when it is suspended, we are no longer in the world but a part of the world. That is what the music of Orpheus did to the women who in a kind of collective trance or ecstasy tore his head off and tossed it into the sea, where it drifted slowly away, still singing.

Eyes

I will never be able to understand how the eyes function. I will never be able to grasp how a reflection of the external world, with all its objects and movements, can flow in through the eyes and be projected as images in the darkness of the mind. I know that the eye consists of a vitreous body, an anterior and a posterior chamber, and a number of membranes. I know that light energy is transformed into nerve impulses when light meets the eye, due to the breakdown of a substance called visual purple, and that these impulses are flung along neural pathways to the visual cortex of the brain, where they are reconstituted as inner perceptions. This process, so infinitely fine-tuned there are more than one hundred and twenty million light-sensitive cells in the retina, is what enabled me to see my daughters playing badminton on the lawn on a warm quiet summer day in July amid motionless green plants and shrubs and trees beneath a blazing blue sky, both their somewhat clumsy movements and the concentrated looks on their faces which now and then dissolved into laughter or accusations. The same process also allowed me to see snow falling in the darkness outside the kitchen window as I stood there early this morning waiting for the coffee to percolate, how the snowflakes, which were small and granular, traced the slightest movement of the air, and one by one settled on, under or between the blades of grass, which now, a few hours later, when the light from the distant sun, much muted by the cloud cover, shines over the landscape, are entirely covered by white snow. I am unable to grasp how it happens, but I could have been satisfied with the explanation that it is simply a matter of mechanics and matter, a pure transfer of energy, a question of atoms and photons, if not for the fact that the eyes not only receive light, they also emit it. What kind of light is that? Oh, it is the light within, the light that shines in all the eyes we meet, known and unknown. The eyes of strangers, for instance on board a packed bus on an autumn afternoon, emit a faint light, more like a barely perceptible glimmer in their grimy faces, and what it reveals is hardly more than that they are alive. But the moment those little lanterns of life are turned towards you, and you look into them, what you see is a particular human being. Maybe you take notice of them, maybe not, in the course of a life we gaze into thousands of eyes, most of them slipping by unperceived, but then suddenly there is something there, in those very eyes, something you want and which you would do almost anything to be close to. What is it? For it isn't the pupils you are seeing then, not the irises nor the whites of the eyes. It is the soul, the archaic light of the soul the eyes are filled with, and to gaze into the eyes of the one you love when love is at its most powerful belongs among the highest joys.

Also by Karl Ove Knausgaard

A Time to Every Purpose Under Heaven
A Death in the Family: My Struggle Book 1
A Man in Love: My Struggle Book 2
Boyhood Island: My Struggle Book 3
Dancing in the Dark: My Struggle Book 4
Some Rain Must Fall: My Struggle Book 5
Home and Away: Writing the Beautiful Game
    (with Fredrik Ekelund)